'I remember a time in my life when there was so much change going on, someone who was deeply worried told me I was bound to have a nervous breakdown. Thankfully I did not, but change is definitely not always easy. A wise friend once told me, "Growing things change and changing things grow." As so many people are fearful and uncertain about change, I love how Sarah reminds us of the beauty of change and the way the Lord carries us through different seasons of our lives, which is so necessary.'
Adrienne Camp, singer-songwriter and author of *In Unison* and *Even Me*

'Change is the unavoidable reality in all of our lives. Whether it's planned or unplanned and unwelcome, we will all experience it on some level or other. In this book, Sarah has articulated some timeless truths in beautiful ways by illustrating it with her own journey, which has been filled with change. I have had the privilege of knowing Sarah since she was a teenager, and watching her life and growth as a follower of Jesus has been truly amazing. She has taken some big steps of faith at a young age and has seen God work in amazing ways. One of the most impressive observations has been watching her navigate these major changes with grace and without bitterness. As I read this book, I found it refreshing, encouraging, honest and inspiring to embrace change with grace, seeing God's guiding hand in it all. This is not a shallow read. It has depth, content and practical application for everyone. I know you will be blessed by time spent in its pages.'
Scott Cunningham
Costa Mesa

'Sarah Yardley is one of the most thoughtful, reflective and engaging leaders I know. She reads widely, thinks deeply and has written a book on one of the most pressing issues of our time.'
Pete Greig, 24-7 Prayer International and Emmaus Road Church

'Apprenticeship to Jesus means we allow Jesus to be our guide as we navigate constant change. Two of the critical ingredients in this journey of becoming are imitation and practice. We need people to emulate and spiritual wisdom, passed on in the form of simple embodied habits, to practise. This book provides that opportunity. If a young person asked me to point them in the direction of someone on fire in their faith, navigating constant change with Jesus and who would be a great example to follow, I would point them straight to Sarah Yardley. This book offers such an example and is packed full of practical wisdom on how to embrace the life-changing adventure of following an unchanging God.'
Pete Hughes, Senior Pastor of King's Cross Church (KXC) in London and author of *All Things New*

'Change is something we all experience, yet many of us struggle to navigate it well. I can't think of anyone better to help us to approach change with a fresh perspective than Sarah, who is one of the most thoughtful, inquisitive, Jesus-centred people I know. By sharing her own experiences of change alongside a wealth of profound biblical reflections, Sarah has gifted us with a timely, wise and joy-filled book that reveals the transforming yet unchanging hope of Jesus in an ever-changing world.'
Ben Jack, Global Head of Advance and author of *My Lord and My God*

'With weight and power, Sarah's words will transform not just your mind but also your heart. Knowledge is available, but revelation is fought for. Sarah shares her revelation with us, and our lives are transformed by her wisdom. I devoured her book!'
Bianca Juarez Olthoff, speaker, pastor and bestselling author of *How to Have Your Life Not Suck*

'I've been hoping Sarah would write a book and am relieved to find that her first of no doubt many is as great as I suspected it would be. Sarah is a lover of words, a deep thinker, a beautiful writer, a theologian and a disciple who really does try to love Jesus with all of who she is, and her neighbours as herself, no matter where she finds them. The way this work journeys through the different colours and dynamics of the changes we face and the invitation to be changed that we find in the process is helpful and hopeful. Anyone in their twenties and thirties will be in a series of life-changing events and decisions, and this little book will be a great companion for the journey, and one I have personally appreciated. Thank you, Sarah, yes for these words, but more for the way you live your life with Jesus through every circumstance.'
Miriam Swanson, Fusion Movement

Sarah Yardley is a Californian based in Cornwall who knows a little something about change, her life carrying her from mega-church to village church, and from home-schooling to visiting more than 90 countries. She is Mission Lead at Creation Fest UK, Canon of Truro Cathedral and on the team at Tubestation, Polzeath. *MORE > Change* is her first book.

MORE>
Change
Navigating change with an unchanging God.

Sarah Yardley

FORM

First published in Great Britain in 2021

Form
36 Causton Street
London SW1P 4ST
www.spck.org.uk

British Library Cataloguing-in-Publication Data
A catalogue record for this book is available from the British Library

ISBN: 978–0–281–08458–6
eBook ISBN: 978–0–281–08459–3

1 3 5 7 9 10 8 6 4 2

Typeset by CRB Associates, Potterhanworth, Lincolnshire
First printed in Great Britain by Ashford Colour Press
eBook by CRB Associates, Potterhanworth, Lincolnshire

Produced on paper from sustainable sources.

To all those seeking grace in change
(may you be found)

Contents

xi Foreword by Evan Wickham

1 Introduction

7 Chapter one: Unchanging God

19 Chapter two: The greatest change

33 Chapter three: Our changing lives

49 Chapter four: Navigating change

61 Chapter five: The pace of change

79 Chapter six: Desiring change

93 Chapter seven: Living in the light of eternal change

107 Chapter eight: Changing the world

116 *Acknowledgements*

118 *References*

Contents

Foreword

Like every other kid in the 1980s, I liked *Back to the Future* movies too much. I turn 40 this year and I'm still waiting for a hoverboard. Meanwhile, our three-bedroom house has four different phone numbers, half a dozen computers and enough mobile learning devices to last another pandemic. My wife and I have one adult child, two teenagers, two little ones and two in heaven. We also lead a church – something I swore as a pastor's kid I'd never do, but I love it.

Change is inevitable.

Today's visionaries predict a future not even Doc Brown saw coming – a future where change is the only constant. Most of what our kids learn in school today will be irrelevant by the year 2050. Historian and atheist Yuval Noah Harari (2018) writes, 'To survive and flourish in such a world, you will ... have to repeatedly let go of some of what you know best, and feel at home with the unknown.'

For an atheist, Harari sounds a lot like Jesus. Let go of some of what you know best. Feel at home with the unknown.

As Sarah Yardley will show you in these pages, part of the brilliance of Christianity is how every generation has to let go of some of what it knows best in order to encounter Jesus afresh. As God's children, we believe that he wants every single one of us to change, to mature in understanding and trust. On the one hand, this means affirming Scripture's authority in our lives, respecting those who came before us and obeying Jesus' teachings in Spirit-driven community. On the other hand, maturity means acknowledging that Christian expression has never been something one generation can crystallize for all posterity. That would create a lazy faith. All we'd need to do is copy and paste from books or reminisce about how our favourite pastor would do it, and that's it. No need for character or maturity. No need for change. The way of Jesus is different. His paradoxical invitation is to find your life by losing it – to 'let go of some of what you know best, and feel at home with the unknown'.

Sarah hasn't just made her home in the unknown. She has also rearranged the furniture, lit a warm fire and set the table for all anxious souls who draw near the door. As if our whole lives we have been apprehensively pacing the front porch, Sarah herein welcomes us over the threshold of the unknown with wild-eyed hospitality.

MORE > Change is not only a book about transience, or spiritual disciplines, or even how to pray, though it's all of those things. I've come to believe that it is more than a book. It is also an invitation to bloom where you are planted in every season, to be a branch that extends from the vine of Jesus' own being so that you lose track of where you end and he begins. To feel at home in every unknown.

I wish this book had existed 15 years ago, for my own sake.

I had just finished reading *MORE > Change* and it made me think about long meals with friends and how to prepare for the unexpected. These thoughts led me to the second chapter of John's Gospel – the story of Jesus changing water to wine. The chapter begins with a wedding that has run dry. Later, Jesus commands the servers to fill jars with water. Jesus changes the water into wine so good that even the banquet master is baffled. The story ends with the author John declaring that this is the first sign to reveal Jesus' glory, resulting in his disciples' trust.

Why water to wine? Scholars suggest best theories and prophetic allusions, but the truth is, anyone who answers definitively is only guessing. Apparently, Jesus likes really good wine and changing things.

But midway through, an extraordinary detail is recorded. Here we see the portrait of Mary, a woman of faith, brimming with intuition. She boldly approaches Jesus, concerned about the wine shortage. Jesus appears to resist her. Mary is unfazed. With eyes fixed on Jesus, she says to the servants, 'Do whatever he tells you.'

There in the middle of Jesus' first sign is a woman who knows that she is fiercely loved, confidently calling others to obey Jesus' voice. Mary doesn't perform the sign but, let's face it – no Mary, no wine. She is confident and catalytic. Don't you long to live in confidence that you are loved by the Maker of the universe? Don't you desire to be a catalyst of Jesus' delight, regardless of what the future holds?

The heart of Sarah Yardley's book is that you can. Starting now, for the rest of your life, you can feel at home in the unknown with someone who loves you enough to die for you. *MORE* > *Change* is an invitation to find your home (again and again) in King Jesus.

Don't rush through this book. Don't harvest data from it. Linger with it. Read one chapter a day, perhaps even the same chapter each day for a week, pausing to invite conversation with the Holy Spirit.

I once told Sarah that she has weathered more change than anyone I have ever met, and managed to do it without cynicism. I know why. She writes – and more importantly *lives* – as someone who knows that she is fiercely loved. In these pages, with her eyes fixed on Jesus, Sarah says to all who stand on the brink of the unknown: 'Do whatever he tells you.'

Evan Wickham
Lead Pastor of Park Hill Church
San Diego, California, 2021

Introduction

The hardest thing about writing a book on change is that almost nothing stays still long enough to capture it easily. This book is not about cementing ideas on change, imprisoning them to a fixed point so that we can look at them every once in a while and comment, 'What nice ideas we have about change! How comfortable they are!'

No, this book is instead an exploration of the way people, places, practices and perspectives are shifted in light of change. Over my 30-odd years of life, I've changed houses, changed countries, changed perspective, changed affections, changed accents. The seed for this book was planted when my friend Evan Wickham commented that I had navigated more change than anyone else he had ever met, and somehow managed to do it without cynicism.

I am not the same person I was when I started writing this book. In the unfolding story of life, we change. There were times when I would have told you with bold confidence that the only constant in change was God's presence in my life – and I would have told you this with a smile on my face and sincerity in my heart. There have been other times when I would have said that same sentence through clenched teeth and any cheer would have been forced at best. Yet, in the words of Viktor Frankl, 'when we are no longer able to change a situation, we are challenged to change ourselves' (Sandberg, 2017).

I personally rarely see change coming. I live in the present moment, in all its grit and glory, and miss the joy of change. I root myself in home, studies, friendships, community and safety, so change can feel like a violent act. And then . . .

Lockdown.
Loss.
Love.
Life happens.

This book is for the ones who choose change and the ones who find change forced on them. It is about living well in times of change. And it's short, because if your life is changing, you're probably living it to the full. It is an honest book, because that's the only way I know how to write. And it's a book about the God who is unchanging in character and love, because the only way I've managed to navigate change without cynicism is by knowing him.

The Bible speaks often of change, of the practice of being made new, describing it in this way in 2 Corinthians 5.17: 'Therefore, if anyone is in Christ, he is a new creation. The old has passed away; behold, the new has come.'

If you grew up anywhere near Christians, you've probably read this verse so many times it has lost any impact. If you grew up in the circles I did, you may even have a backpack with a butterfly and the words 'New creation' or perhaps a coffee mug, keychain, pencil or journal. And somehow, in the midst of all the trinkets, it's easy to miss the whole point of this short scripture. Jesus didn't come to make us better. He came to make us new. The most dramatic change of our lives occurs the day we meet him, and someone had the brilliant idea to turn that inexpressible concept into a backpack.

In reality, the picture of a new creation is bigger than caterpillar to butterfly, but let's start with that one, because it works. First of all, what kind of God is creative and outrageous enough to link the two? A fuzzy, creeping, crawly creature turns into a winged beauty. It gives shape to so many other pictures of change in our lives.

On a scientific level, the process is even more extraordinary. I'm not a scientist, but I did teach science to 12-year-old boys for a year and some of it stuck (with me, anyway – I'm not sure about them). When a caterpillar is in the chrysalis, its guts literally change shape. They become narrower and shorter while the breathing tubes expand. It's as though the internal system of the caterpillar is reorganized and restructured so that it can live in a new and soaring way. The new creation is beautiful, but the process can be a little bit messy.

Our world is in a long season of change. At times, this change is to be celebrated: the ending of apartheid, the vote for women in most countries, consistent opportunities for education, a web of connectedness that allows me to keep in touch equally with my sister in Amman and my family in California, while living in a town in Cornwall, England.

At other times, change is catastrophic: the horrors of genocide and war, the heartbreak of millions still living in slavery, the oppression of racism, the tragedy of natural disasters and the endless uncertainty of political debates. The same technology that connects us can also drive a wedge of division between us. Change divides our generations; those of an older generation may struggle to grasp the changes of this brave new world and mindset, and the younger generation often does too. Concern about poor mental health is at an all-time high, and there is an increasing craving for stability and rootedness in all generations.

How do we navigate change and restlessness?

I'd like to invite you to consider the way that the Bible speaks about change. It speaks about new life often. For those of us who follow Jesus, our invitation is to embrace change. That's easier said than done. I still believe that we navigate change primarily by looking to Jesus. We are told that he is the same yesterday, today and for ever. We'll explore that concept further in the book, but I believe that many of the principles of navigating change are true regardless of the chapter we are living in. The invitation of God's Word, living and powerful, is to trust that God has given us all that will be necessary for our spiritual journey as we become more and more like Christ.

Change can feel daunting. Like the caterpillar, we can sense that our guts are literally being reshaped, and we're not at all certain we signed up for this. There are two alternatives we face as we navigate seasons of change: despairing cynicism or hopeful expectation. These words are written to guide us to hopeful expectation that even when change is hard, God is good.

As we consider the people, places, practices and perspectives that shape us, I pray we discover a fresh hope and expectation that God is *with* us. As C. S. Lewis writes in his classic book *Mere Christianity* (1996):

> Imagine yourself as a living house. God comes in to rebuild that house. At first, perhaps, you can understand what He is doing. He is getting the drains right and stopping the leaks in the roof and so on; you knew that those jobs needed doing and so you are not surprised. But presently He starts knocking the house about in a way that hurts abominably and does not seem to make any sense. What on earth is He up to? The explanation is that He is building quite a different house from the one you thought of – throwing out a new wing here, putting on an extra floor there, running up towers, making courtyards. You thought you were being made into a decent little cottage: but He is building a palace. He intends to come and live in it Himself.

The steadfast love of the LORD never ceases; his mercies never come to an end.

(Lamentations 3.22)

Chapter one

UNCHANGING GOD

It is likely that you are navigating some significant life changes right now and are looking for specific answers in the pages of this book. Yet, if three decades of following Jesus has taught me anything, it is that the first step in searching for answers is to look at him – at his endless love, power and wisdom.

It may be that, like me, you grew up singing so many scriptures, you have found them embedded deeply in your heart and mind (or it may be that the only tunes you hum were written by Taylor Swift). The one that opens this chapter has an easy chorus I grew up singing – so simple I can't write these words without humming it to myself. I wish my hums stayed in tune; that's a gift I have yet to receive but, as it turns out, the words are true even when my pitch is off-key. The ongoing story of Scripture is the story of the God who loved us and came to us. His love towards us is an unchanging story, not shaped by the weight of our circumstances, worries, uncertainty or confusion.

I first grasped this truth at the age of nine, when I had my first real crisis of faith. Like many, I started asking most of my big questions early in life. I think that we would do well to listen to the questions of children. Some are haphazard, but they often represent a genuine searching, and if that searching is met with silence, it can extend to an adult expectation that God is silent as well. My crisis boiled down to this simple question: 'Am I only a Christian because I've been born into a Christian family? If I was born in India, would I be Hindu? If I'd been born in in Dubai, would I be Muslim?' As an adult, I can now extend that question: 'If I was born in Europe, would I be an atheist? If I was born in twenty-first-century America, an intelligent agnostic?'

At the time of my wondering, my dad was working on an all-night prayer line hosted by our church. He'd go in and answer the calls of people who wanted to pray with someone, even if it was the middle of the night – perhaps especially because it was the middle of the night. Although my mum was right to be suspicious that I was just trying to avoid bedtime, she let me call my dad that night. I still remember twisting my finger round the cord of the telephone, stammering out my question, and, decades later, I still remember my dad's clear response, walking me through a series of questions:

Do you believe there is a God or that we are here by accident?

If there is such a God, is he a God of love?

If a God of love, would he choose to reveal himself?

My nine-year-old self hoped the affirmative to all three, which led us to a discussion around the three ancient religions (Hinduism, Buddhism and Judaism as a foundation for Christian faith). Of the three, we discussed the specific beauty of the Judeo-Christian faith as the one where God came to us, extended his life in love and gave us the unearned favour and kindness of new life. In short, my dad spoke to me about grace.

That conversation was the first time I remember grasping faith on an intellectual level. Considering God is an eternal preoccupation, not one that we will finish in even our earthly lifetime, but the way I began to grasp the love of God was new to me. It caught me off guard, this bewildering kindness. I've walked with Jesus now for most of my life, and the reality of that opening verse has been continually true – the steadfast love of the Lord never ceases.

This truth is especially important in an ever-changing world. We change habits, friends, clothing, hair, work, love. If the room is too warm, we can change the temperature. If a relationship becomes toxic, we can change our commitment. In some ways, change is so easy for us that the concept of an unchanging God requires a shift in perspective.

God's unchanging character towards us is part of his own nature. An earlier generation of writers would have called these the 'attributes' of God. That word has fallen out of fashion, but the ideas have not. Let's consider together four attributes of the unchanging God who I fell in love with at the age of nine. I have not yet recovered from the fall.

ENDLESSLY LOVING

The love of God is described in many ways: patient and kind, eternally powerful, sacrificial, active, gentle (see 1 Corinthians 13; Romans 8.38–39; John 15.13; 1 John 3.18; Ephesians 4.2). A whole chapter in 1 Corinthians 13 is dedicated to the love of God, describing it in this way in verses 4–7:

Love is patient and kind; love does not envy or boast; it is not arrogant or rude. It does not insist on its own way; it is not irritable or resentful; it does not rejoice at wrongdoing, but rejoices with the truth. Love bears all things, believes all things, hopes all things, endures all things.

One of the reasons we have such a difficult time grasping the reality of God's love is that it is so different from the love we tend to see reflected in our culture. Much of our love is dependent on *our* actions, relationships, generosity or attitudes. The love of God is wholly other to this. It does not rely on our actions or attitudes; it is an unchanging love regardless of what our lives look like.

When our lives change, it can knock our confidence and certainty. During the first lockdown period related to COVID, many of us had the rug pulled out from beneath our feet. During that time of change, in which the whole world pressed pause and no one was an expert, I found myself having internal wrestling matches around purpose, relationships and commitment. The one place that I found peace was when I stopped, took a deep breath and simply spent time with the God who I am confident loves me with an unchanging love.

The God of the Bible is endlessly loving, but it is with a jealous love. An author who wrote a book on the nature and character of this God of love describes that jealous love in this way:

> It is a strange and beautiful eccentricity of the free God that He has allowed His heart to be emotionally identified with men. Self-sufficient as He is, He wants our love and will not be satisfied till He gets it. Free as He is, He has let His heart be bound to us forever.
> (Tozer, 1978)

In other words, this unchanging love is not a robotic or abstract love, disconnected from any form of emotion or affection. The pursuing love of God is shown to us most brilliantly in the person and work of Jesus, who came to live among us as God incarnate. The unchanging God chose to dwell in a body with fingernails and earwax, to experience the bumps and bruises of a life of carpentry, to develop blisters and calluses, to laugh and love and live among those he created. Ultimately, the purpose of his life was to give it, in true sacrificial love, through his death on the cross. In doing so, as Tozer wrote, he let his heart be bound to us for ever, and continually invites us to respond by giving him our love.

ENDLESSLY POWERFUL

When we think of power, we don't always think of beauty. Power used in the wrong way causes the horror of the Holocaust, the pain of subjugation, the frustration of corruption. Set aside those ideas for a moment to consider the difference between a holy power and a corrupt power. Holy power is reflected in the God who spoke and the worlds were formed (Genesis 1.1). It is shown in the one who commands the morning and causes the dawn to know its place (Job 38.12), the one who puts understanding in our minds (Job 38.36), who makes all things possible (Matthew 19.26).

The power of God is called his *omnipotence* or, to say it in more common language, he is all-powerful. This idea has led to endless jokes and riddles, including the question: 'Can God create a stone so heavy that he cannot lift it?' Try it out at your next party. It almost always provokes an interesting conversation. I appreciate the way C. S. Lewis (1966) approaches this idea: 'Omnipotence means power to do all that is intrinsically possible, not to do the intrinsically impossible. You may attribute miracles to him, but not nonsense. This is no limit to his power.'

The endlessly powerful nature of God should be held with the reality of his endless love towards us. Yet, like any good father, this one doesn't just magically give his children whatever they want. We want God's power to be shown in ways that are practically helpful, with a fairy-tale ending. We want the pumpkin to become a chariot, the worn-out slipper to become glass, the perfect partner to pursue us and the pains and worries of life to effortlessly disappear. The power of God is not the power of a fairy godmother or a genie in a bottle. Instead, the power of God brings about the rising of the sun (and his mercies are new every morning). The power of God is in his presence with us (and a peace that passes understanding). The power of God is revealed in the way he works all things together for good (to those who love him and are called according to his purposes). The power of God is seen less in changing our circumstances and more in changing our souls. We change habits, friends, clothing, hair, work, love. God changes hearts, minds, attitudes and souls.

ENDLESSLY WISE

One of my favourite passages of Scripture describes the wisdom of God in this way:

'pure, then peaceable, gentle, open to reason, full of mercy and good fruits, impartial and sincere' (James 3.17).

I pray often for this kind of wisdom in my own life. One of the most astounding realities of the character of God is that, as we walk with and know him, he gives us his own character. The endless wisdom of God means that, in times of change, he knows what is best for us and our souls. What is best is often different from what we would choose. I have seen that many of my unanswered prayers were not wise prayers. An all-knowing, endlessly wise God understands far more than we do about our lives and circumstances.

In Ecclesiastes, we read that 'the advantage of knowledge is that wisdom preserves the life of him who has it' (7.12). The endless wisdom of God preserves our lives, often guarding us from the pitfalls that we're not even aware are before us. Years ago, I started a job that I thought was my dream role, the place where I would stay for life. For a number of reasons the job disappeared and I wrestled with God for months. I doubted his wisdom, his knowledge and his love. Over a decade later, I can see so many reasons why that job wasn't right. It would have taken my life down a completely different pathway. The wisdom of God has preserved and ultimately extended my life, even when I wasn't able to see it.

ENDLESSLY THE SAME

The idea of endless 'sameness' calls to mind robotic assembly lines, boring factories, the couple who have grown together in so many ways that they've lost track of where to even start a conversation (and they probably look alike as well). The theological word for the 'sameness' of God is 'immutability'. He is the 'Father of

lights, with whom there is no variation or shadow due to change'
(James 1.17).

This unchanging nature of God is anything but boring. If you're in
a chapter of change, you may or may not find it beautiful, but
in many ways we are conditioned to expect change. We look for
the newest film, the most recent beauty product, the just-released
phone model, the current podcast, always ready for a new idea to
entertain us. The endlessly same God is wholly other and beautiful
in a different way.

When we come to Jesus in petulant worry, he responds with
grace.
When our world is falling apart and our way is unclear, God
gives us hope.
When our friends have failed us and our relationships are rocky,
our God is solid.
When we lack direction and feel lost, the Spirit is still speaking.
When our hearts change, wander and fail, our God is the one
who runs after us, prepares a meal and welcomes us home.

The unchanging nature of our God means that we never have to
wonder if he wants to hear from us, never need doubt that our
failures have separated us, never need worry that love has been lost
because of our uncertainty. Sometimes we are lost more than we
are found. Such is grace.

KNOWING GOD

Knowing God in times of change means we return, over and over again, to what we know to be true of his character, regardless of our feelings. Where our feelings would otherwise dictate our decisions, we instead choose to believe in the love, the power, the wisdom and the unchanging nature of God as more powerful than our circumstances.

I hope this short chapter might encourage you to start or continue a conversation with God about these things. If you'd like, feel free to use the following prayer as a starting point.

Eternal God,

I come to you today, wondering. My life is full of change, and you are the God who does not change. I ask for your presence with me, for the peace of your Holy Spirit to be seen in my life and my circumstances.

As I consider who you are, I pray that the reality of your love would be real to me in a new way today. Thank you that you chose to love me, even though I never could have earned or deserved it. I invite your love to shine into the darkened spaces of my heart. I turn from the things that distract me from your love and turn towards you.

I pray that I would know your power in my pain, your wisdom in my questions and your constancy in my restlessness. I invite your Spirit to make me more like Jesus, even in the places where I don't yet understand.

Amen.

FURTHER READING

Lewis, C. S. (1966) *The Problem of Pain* (London and Glasgow: Fontana).

Packer, J. I. (2005) *Knowing God* (London: Hodder & Stoughton).

Tozer, A. W. (1978) *The Knowledge of the Holy* (New York: HarperCollins).

Wilkin, Jen (2016) *None Like Him* (Wheaton, IL: Crossway).

I know a man of such mildness
and kindness it is trying to
change my life. He does not
preach, teach, but simply is.
It is astonishing, for he is Christ's
ambassador truly, by rule and act.
But, more, he is kind with the
sort of kindness that shines
out, but is resolute, not fooled.
He has eaten the dark hours and
could also, I think, soldier for
God, riding out under the storm
clouds, against the world's pride
and unkindness, with both
unassailable sweetness, and
tempering word.

(Oliver, 2006)

Chapter two

THE GREATEST CHANGE

Change happens in our lives the way we fall in love: sometimes slowly, sometimes all at once. Followers of Jesus love to celebrate the all-at-once stories, the instant transformations, the chrysalis unfolding to reveal the butterfly. We love these stories because they showcase the grandeur of a miracle-working God, they thrill our senses, strengthen our faith, look good from our stages. But the longer I walk with Jesus and others, the more I recognize that the story is often a slow unfolding, a long obedience in the same direction, a quiet and hidden change.

When I tell my own story of finding faith, I can see four places where my life changed. First, I was born into a home where Jesus was loved and honoured, and I can't remember ever feeling any differently. Next, I had an intellectual crisis of faith at the age of nine and decided that following Jesus made the most sense. At the age of 16, I recognized that obedience to this God would cost me something, and the sacrifice was worth the decision. When I was 25 years old, I had a radical and transformative experience of grace, and I fell in love with Jesus. If you were to ask me which of these was my greatest change, I would struggle to select just one of these experiences as the definitive one. These and a thousand others shaped my heart and changed my soul. Our hearts change in ways that we cannot control, and the most significant changes can happen in the quietest of moments.

The greatest change is the one that happens when we truly encounter Jesus. No one ever came into his presence and left the same. Some adored and followed, some laughed and rejected, some wondered and dallied, some loved and forgot, but no one could ignore the force of his presence. In this chapter, we will look at three stories of the way Jesus changed lives in parallel with the stories of three friends of mine. May we be captivated, charmed and entranced by the life of Jesus.

NEW LIFE AND POWER

Perhaps the most well known of the stories of change in Scripture is the story found in John chapter 3. A religious leader named Nicodemus has come to Jesus by night, searching for a sign that Jesus is different, other, the one who carries the presence of God. Jesus responds, as his opening line, with these rather bewildering words: 'Truly, truly, I say to you, unless one is born again, he cannot see the kingdom of God' (verse 3). Try that line out next time you're in a pub or coffee shop; it's just as confusing in our day as it must have been to Nicodemus at the time. Their conversation continues, a back-and-forth on the practical and biological challenges of re-entering our mother's womb. Don't overvisualize this; it's not a pretty picture. Ultimately, Jesus is leading Nicodemus to a spiritual reality, and Nicodemus keeps returning to the logistics.

One of my most dramatic experiences of seeing new life took place in the Dominican Republic. I was leading a team of 74 on a short-term mission trip from my church, and I was in charge of all the logistics. We had schedules, itineraries, dramatic presentations, Spanish songs; in short, I had ticked all the boxes. There was only one problem, which I realized when we arrived in the country. A select few of my team, in the country on mission, were not yet followers of Jesus themselves. One or two actually hated God, but they didn't want to miss out on a week's adventure in the Caribbean with all their friends. As any naïve Christian leader would be, I was shocked, speechless. When one of them turned to me on the bus and told me about his lack of faith, I did manage to say, 'But the toys and the treats we are bringing will only last a few days; if you're not here to tell them about life in Jesus, what will you give that will last more than a moment?' We then exited the bus and he played the character of Death in one of our drama presentations. The irony is not lost on me, years later.

I began to pray for this particular group of young people; they were influential and popular, and I didn't know how to reach their hearts. They had heard all the words, knew all the stories, but they were stuck on the logistics. Towards the end of the trip, I was sitting with one member of the group on the stairs, and he was speaking of his anger and then, unexpectedly, he simply began to weep. He said to me and his friends, 'Jesus died for me and I have never chosen to see his love for me.'

His group of friends and I went to an upper room just above us, and this young man repented of his sin and gave his life to God. One by one, each of his friends did the same. The room was full of the presence and power of the Spirit of God. We were praying and singing long into the night, and while life has not been without its challenges for each of them, I watched five young men and women enter the kingdom of God that night, born again.

In the conversation between Jesus and Nicodemus, Jesus says these words:

'The wind blows where it wishes, and you hear its sound, but you do not know where it comes from or where it goes. So it is with everyone who is born of the Spirit' (John 3.8).

When change comes through the power of the Holy Spirit, it often comes in ways that are beyond our own power or control;

it cannot be manipulated by our logistics. In many ways, the work of the Spirit is still a mystery to me after decades of walking with Jesus. It's a beautiful mystery, the kind that reminds me new life is a gift, and the giver is good. Have you noticed how change comes in ways that we never expected, and in ways that we did not expect would be a gift? Allowing our lives to be led by the Spirit causes us to be surprised by the unexpected beauty of a change that is greater than we can plan on our own.

NEW LIFE AND MYSTERY

The next incident of life change we see in John's Gospel happens between Jesus and a woman from Samaria. Throughout the Gospels, we see Jesus interacting with women over and over again, breaking the expectations of a patriarchal society, elevating the person and identity of those who were often forgotten. In John chapter 4, we find Jesus, sitting alone by the well, wearied from a long journey, catching a few minutes of quiet while his followers have gone to find food. A woman comes to draw water from the well, and Jesus engages her in a conversation in which he reveals spiritual truth, historical wisdom and practical insight into her life. In short, she has been looking for love in all the wrong places, hoping that one of these relationships might change her life, and Jesus says to her that 'whoever drinks of the water that I will give . . . will never be thirsty again' (verse 14).

Our lives are one long search for living water. One of my friends who has been searching is a radiant, articulate, expressive surfer. We met at a dance showcase and loved each other at first sight. For several years, we have journeyed through doubts and questions, big ideas and small decisions, what it means to live in great gladness in light of the world's great need.[1] A year into our friendship, she wrote me a five-page letter about what it has meant to encounter God as Father, the one who loves her unconditionally, unlike her earthly father. Her identity, as abused, abandoned, used and objectified, is melting away slowly and, above all, her new identity in Christ is *loved*.

One icy November, she chose to be baptized in the sea she loves so much. God still speaks to her in many ways: through the moon, a moth, a parable or a puppy. Over the years, I've seen her life change in slow but beautiful ways. The pain that once defined her became a catalyst for her to enter training and begin to support others in their place of pain and trauma. The God she once felt abandoned and rejected by became to her a place of love and comfort. She is, above all, honest.

In the conversation of Jesus with the woman at the well, Jesus says these words to her: 'true worshipers will worship the Father in spirit and truth, for the Father is seeking such people to worship him' (John 4.23). I have spent much of my life with Jesus seeking instantaneous change for his followers, expecting that, from the moment they know him, their lives will be completely transformed.

---

1   An idea from the writings of Frederick Buechner (1993) *Wishful Thinking* (San Francisco, CA: HarperSanFrancisco), pp. 118–19.

Walking with my friend has helped me to stop, breathe, see that, at times, our heart change is a result of walking by the Spirit and choosing truth. There is beauty in the mystery of the long, slow story of seeing change unfold.

Choose a point in your life two years ago. Think about the friends, the choices, the ideas, the location that shaped you. Identify several ways you have changed since then. We so often look at our stories in the vibrant now rather than in the overarching narrative. Ask yourself: have I changed in ways that reflect a heart turned towards Jesus? Am I choosing to walk in spirit and in truth?

NEW LIFE AND DISAPPOINTMENT

Writing on the greatest change – the way that we become more like Jesus as we surrender our lives to his love – would not feel honest without asking: why can change take so long? What about when we are disappointed? It is a great mistake to read the Gospels and imagine that Jesus and the disciples soared from glory to glory, living on the mountains and avoiding the valleys. We read in the book of Hebrews that:

'we do not have a high priest who is unable to sympathize with our weaknesses, but one who in every respect has been tempted as we are, yet without sin' (Hebrews 4.15).

Jesus knew the weight of disappointment, discouragement and dismay, and did not avoid the hard conversations. Shortly after talking with the woman at the well, Jesus encounters 'a multitude of invalids – blind, lame, and paralyzed. One man . . . had been an invalid for thirty-eight years' (John 5.3–5). Let's not brush past this detail in the text. Here, we find a multitude of disappointments, hopes that have been raised and dashed over and over again, hearts with a protective shell built around them to guard against yet another promise unfulfilled. Living in the unanswered can lead us towards bitterness and cynicism as self-protection. We insulate our souls against yet another weary loss.

This makes the question Jesus asks the man even more surprising, seeing that he has been there for many years: 'Do you want to be healed?' Perhaps Jesus is challenging his expectations. Perhaps he is asking whether or not he is now happy to be defined by his disappointment. Either way, the man answers by giving his list of excuses for why he has not yet been healed: the people who have let him down, the circumstances that have limited him, the freedom he has seen in others.

I know a young man with crosses tattooed on his wrists. He's taken a few bad turns and had a few bad turns made for him. He owes money to dealers, his life is achingly messed up, he spirals in and out of *wanting* a new life. Not long ago, I prayed with him, listened as he said sorry to God for 19 years of sin and heartbreak, much of it the circumstances he has been in, but enough of it his choice. He had that vocabulary I have so often heard with new Christians, where somehow they know how to speak of faith even though they haven't lived it yet, like a spiritual language, given as a gift.

The very next day, he was raging, violent, out of control. I have seen miraculous, instantaneous transformation. I have watched people step from darkness into light, from bondage into freedom, from the sins that so easily beset them into power, but it's easy to forget the verses that speak of the costly, sacrificial, unexpected, messy, bumbling journey where Jesus asks us this simple question: 'Do you want to be healed?' Because if you do, it will cost you everything. It won't be an instant fix. And it might hurt more in the short term than the sticking plaster you are wearing on your soul. My friend is still deciding his answer to that question. I hope it won't take 38 years.

In the Gospel story, Jesus commands healing and it is done. But his words to this man are sobering: 'See, you are well! Sin no more, that nothing worse may happen to you' (John 5.14). Do not read this and hear: if you sin, that will immediately carry a vindictive consequence. Remember, all is grace. But in the mystery of new life, as we wrestle with disappointment and unanswered questions, one of the beauties of the gospel is that we are still given a measure of choice, and we choose every day whether to wake up and look to Jesus or, instead, turn back to our own crutches, safety nets and coping mechanisms.

What happens when we look to Jesus? I have found, over and over again, that the words of Psalm 34.4–5 are true:

> I sought the LORD, and he answered me
>   and delivered me from all my fears.
> Those who look to him are radiant,
>   and their faces shall never be ashamed.

One of our greatest fears ought to be the fear of 'misliving'. It's a word we don't use often, but I have incorporated it into my vocabulary to remind me that every day we make choices about how we live in light of the change that comes through being loved by God, our Father, being redeemed by Jesus and being led by the Spirit of a living God. We mislive when we allow the ideas, the temptations, the discouragements and the uncertainties of our world to shape our hearts. Looking to Jesus is our daily invitation to seek first the kingdom of God, expect deliverance from our fears and find radiant hope and freedom from shame in his presence. When we do these things, we live in expectation.

NEW LIFE AND AUTHORITY

The greatest change happens when we walk in new life. Remember, Jesus did not come to make us better people, but to make us new people. Your life might include a radical and instantaneous change, a slow and beautiful falling in love or echoes of disappointment and past hurt. Mine includes all three, in different chapters. If we live by the emotion of our story, we can find ourselves in a whirling vortex of opinion and advice. I anchor my soul in this truth from John's Gospel:

'Truly, truly, I say to you, whoever hears my word and believes him who sent me has eternal life. He does not come into judgment, but has passed from death to life' (John 5.24).

This new life gives us new authority. For years, Meghan Markle was a television actress, best known for her role in the series *Suits*. She was reasonably respected, occasionally photographed, comfortably paid. Then she met, fell in love with and married Prince Harry. In a day, she went from being a person with a small measure of authority to one with significant authority. In an interesting turn of events, she and Harry have chosen to rescind much of that authority since that time, but at the moment of her marriage, Meghan was the same person, with the same character, identity and skills, but her position changed when she publicly proclaimed her commitment.

The invitation of Jesus is to hear the Word of God and to believe that in him is eternal life. When we make this commitment, our position changes – from one who would otherwise be under the judgement of God to one who has received eternal life. This changes our position to one with the authority to walk in freedom of identity, freedom from fear, freedom to love. One of the most joyful adventures of the Christian journey is to discover what we are free *for*. We tend to spend much of our time and conversation on what we have been freed from, but the reality is that we are freed to live as sons and daughters of the already, not-yet kingdom of God, to be the ones who whisper and shout that there is a better life than the one our world can sell us, to live the reality of change for our friends and family.

We are not better people; we are new people. We don't work for faith; we work from faith. We don't follow the rules; we follow a good leader. In the words of E. Stanley Jones (1981), 'The new law was a Life. This lifted goodness out of legalism and based it on love.' The greatest change is a life shaped by love, radiant to all.

My Father,

I see the way you are changing me, making me new. I thank you for my own story, for the way you broke into my heart and robbed me of sin, setting me free. I thank you for the way I have seen you work in the lives of others, and for the power of changed lives and instantaneous transformation.

I see so much unfinished work around me. I pray that you would show me where you are already at work, and how you are inviting me to enter in. I ask that my life would radiate the hope of the one who makes all things new.

Guard me from creating a list of rules and logistics to make obedience a task. Help me to walk in such overflowing love for you that my life is lived from delight, not duty. I pray for your Spirit's presence and power to do what is impossible without your life. Thank you for changing my position from judgement and death to life, expectation and hope through Jesus. May I be captivated, charmed and entranced by your love today.

Amen.

FURTHER READING

Buechner, Frederick (2009) *The Alphabet of Grace* (New York: HarperOne).

Keller, Timothy (2014) *Encounters with Jesus* (London: Hodder & Stoughton).

Nouwen, Henri (2016) *Life of the Beloved* (London: Hodder & Stoughton).

Stories of change

Bennett, David (2018) *A War of Loves* (Grand Rapids, MI: Zondervan).

Cook, Becket (2019) *A Change of Affection* (Nashville, TN: Thomas Nelson).

Hoadley Dick, Lois (1984) *Amy Carmichael: Let the little children come* (Chicago, IL: Moody Publishers).

Kuhn, Isobel (2005) *By Searching* (Milton Keynes: Authentic).

McGahan, Anna (2019) *Metanoia* (Sydney: Acorn Press).

Pullinger, Jackie (2006) *Chasing the Dragon* (London: Hodder & Stoughton).

And we all, with unveiled face, beholding the glory of the Lord, are being transformed into the same image from one degree of glory to another. For this comes from the Lord who is the Spirit.

(2 Corinthians 3.18)

Chapter three

OUR CHANGING LIVES

When I think of the many ways my life has changed, I always look back and wish I had grasped even a glimpse of the glory that God was working in me. At the time, it usually felt either messy, uncomfortable, uncertain or casual. It was only with the clarity of time that I could see the transforming glory, but as Kierkegaard (1997) wrote in 1843, 'life must be understood backwards ... But ... it must be lived forwards.'

Change has come in many shapes: change of affection, change of employment, change of understanding, change of heart, change of country, change of friendships, change of pace. I write about our changing lives as one who is still learning to embrace change with grace. At times, when I want to anchor myself in the safe present, I imagine a world where nothing ever changes. Every day, we eat the same meals, wear the same clothes, see the same people, walk the same paths. No new life can enter this world. It is stale and safe. I imagine my own life without change. I never move, never change jobs, never fall in love, never learn or grow. My life is never reshaped by the endless tide of circumstances and events outside of my control. I am the captain of my own destiny and it is exceedingly stable.

Some love change. Some hate it. But when faced with the paradox of these two options: always change or never change, we choose change, every time. We want love, life, the breathtaking uncertainty of the unexpected. We don't want to play it safe and miss the raw and unfiltered reality of an uncertain world.

For the followers of Jesus, change carries a deeper promise. It is the promise that the story is not yet finished, the chapters are still in progress, the ending is both known and surprising, the vast and beautiful truths of grace are yet new. It is the promise that we are being transformed from one degree of glory to another, and that the power of the Spirit of God is at work in our lives – on the paths we know we have chosen and in the unmarked paths of grace.

THREE PLACES OF CHANGE

In this chapter, I will explore three places of change in my life and the way those stories shaped my expectations of change. Each was associated with a specific reality of God's Spirit speaking and leading me in ways that I never would have expected. For those facing the question of change in ways that feel unknown, I hope these stories and the ways they shaped my heart will help pivot theirs towards grace.

A change of calling

I never imagined that I would be involved with teens, travel or mentoring. My own teen years were afflicted with glasses, braces, always being right and home-school jokes. Most of our family holidays were an extension of our dad's business trips, which meant that we usually stayed in a hotel in Las Vegas or Arizona while he worked with local businesses and hotels. Our church had a robust style of Bible teaching, but intentional and individual mentoring were rarer. I only ended up on the trip to Mexico because I was saying goodbye to my sister in a car park attached to the warehouse where I usually worked 60-plus hours each week. I took a break from my work to wave goodbye to the group of teens she was taking across the border when one of the leaders mentioned that there was an extra seat in the van. I had just enough time to drive home, grab a passport and toothbrush, and join them for the weekend, if I was interested.

It was out of character for me at the time, but I did grab my passport and toothbrush, and joined the trip. Instead of changing the lives of others, I found my own life changed by the pace of a different culture, the power of answered prayer and the remarkable honesty and transparency of 32 people joining together for a single purpose. That spontaneous decision launched me into a chapter of passionate dedication to young people, mission trips and intentional mentoring. One seemingly insignificant moment pivoted my whole trajectory.

In some ways, I experienced a sense of my own calling during that trip. It wasn't distinct or audible, but it was clear. It would be years before any of these things became part of my paid vocational work, but there was the spark of passion, and that spark, when tended, became a flame. Pay attention to your sparks. It can be easy to dismiss and bury your dreams, to smother them with practical decisions and procedures.

We can even choose to spiritualize this dismissal and associate the idea of sacrifice and suffering exclusively with the call of God. There is always a downward mobility to the life following Jesus; in Mark 10.45 we see that 'even the Son of Man came not to be served but to serve, and to give his life as a ransom for many'. The life of Jesus was one of continual, joyful service; in the words of Rabindranath Tagore, 'I slept and dreamt that life was joy. / I awoke and saw that life was service. / I acted and behold, service was joy' (Lamott, 2012). I have found that there is always a joy in our obedience to Jesus. If you give your life to God and he calls you to Africa, he will also give you a great love for Africa. When my call was widened to an investment in teens, travel and mentoring, God widened my heart for each of these things as well. They were not a duty; they were a delight.

Oswald Chambers (2017) wrote it this way: 'Faith never knows where it is being led, but it loves and knows the One Who is leading.' If you are unsure of your ultimate calling or the place of your great gladness, the best thing to do is to grow in love and knowledge of Jesus. It is in knowing him that you will grow in confidence, certainty and clarity, and until you know the place where you are called to invest, the simple command to each of us is simply to love our God and love the person nearest to us. If you keep yourself committed to these two things, you will never lack the opportunity to love.

A change of heart

I grew up knowing Scripture. My pastor taught from Genesis through to Revelation, proclaiming 'the whole counsel of God'. I could tell you not just the stories of the patriarchs but also those of the radical woman who hammered a tent peg into the head of an enemy, the rebellious son who caught his hair in a tree, the naked prophets, the fiery visions, the endless parables. I have more Scripture memorized than most, simply because I heard the words read over me every Sunday morning, Sunday night and Wednesday night for decades. My head is full of biblical truth.

When truth makes the 18-inch journey from head to heart, it reshapes our souls. I wanted that journey to happen, prayed for it, cried about it, read every book I could find, served in ministry, became a leader. It took my leaving that familiar place where Scripture was taught so well to discover grace. Perhaps I was so well versed in Scripture that it was too safe; perhaps I wasn't listening. Perhaps even trying to discern why years later shows how little I still know of grace.

Grace found me in Carpinteria, California. I worked with a church by the sea, for a pastor who surfed, with a community who loved well. I left my places of safety and security, my family in every sense of the word, to build a new home, and in that process my soul was awakened to the simple reality of God's great and unearned favour towards me. When I wasn't looking, it found me.

I spent only three months in that happy place. A series of events, including the pastor's daughter being diagnosed with life-threatening cancer, paired with a previously planned round-the-world trip with my sister, meant that I left after an absurdly short amount of time. However, the depth of our stories and the change God can bring aren't based on our own timelines. I have carried the deep intimacy of a new relationship with Jesus from that place into every future chapter of my life.

One of the most significant changes from that time was this very simple truth: Jesus calls us to be *with* him (Mark 3.14). Or, to put it in the words of my pastor, Britt Merrick (2014), 'all ministry flows from intimacy'. This changes our relationship with God from one of obligated servant to that of intimate friend. An intimate friend will still choose obedience, sacrifice and commitment, but those choices flow from a place of love. My heart changed from conscript to lover of Jesus during those months.

A second change was the experience of being captivated, charmed and entranced by the gospel. When we invite others to a life of following Jesus, we want to share why this is not just a good or better life, but the best life we know. Hearing Scripture framed from the perspective of the pursuing love of Jesus, as the story told from the first page to the last, gave me a great passion for inviting others into that story out of delight rather than duty. As my pastor often signed his emails, I learned to quite simply 'enjoy Jesus'.

A change of heart is at the centre of this book's focus. It cannot be manipulated, planned or strategized; it is an act of the Spirit of God who transforms us from glory to glory. When we receive the grace of Christ and the filling of the Spirit, we are made both new and free, because we discover again that it is not our own wisdom or strength that brings our salvation.

Years after this change of heart, I met with my pastor, Britt Merrick, in London. He sent me this blessing; may it be a gift to you as it was to me.

May the nearness of Christ be your good and may you find fullness of joy in him and may the joy of the Lord be your strength. He is your God who daily bears your burdens.

A change of direction

If only we read Scripture and simply obeyed! We read over and over again a very simple word: PRAY. We are told to:

'pray without ceasing' (1 Thessalonians 5.17), 'pray for those who persecute you' (Matthew 5.44), 'pray to your Father' (Matthew 6.6), 'pray and seek my face' (2 Chronicles 7.14), 'pray for one another' (James 5.16), 'pray earnestly' (Matthew 9.38).

After returning from my round-the-world trip to 34 countries, which resulted in my sister coming home with a future husband and both of us with full passports, I was adrift. My heart wanted to return to Carpinteria, but it wasn't the right time and I wandered into a period of depression. I lay in bed for hours. I cried. I didn't know how to function. In my spare time, I organized a few mission trips, because I still loved teens, travel and mentoring, but none of that was paid work. I had a few potential job offers, but nothing made my heart sing. I was 26 years old and lost.

Like any good American, I decided to go and spend a summer in New York. I remember speaking to countless friends about feeling as though I was drifting. Many told me that they would pray for me (and I am certain they did; no one ever says those words and forgets to pray . . . right?). I spent time in Brooklyn and the Upper West Side, hopping to any apartment that could cram me into a corner or offer me a couch. I went to the McQueen exhibition with a group of models, walked miles each day, read books about purpose and direction, helped with a holiday club at Redeemer Church, ate the best empanadas of my life.

One day, my phone rang. On the other end of the line was a pastor named Ken Graves. His voice is so deep you shiver and his life is deeper still. He asked me what was happening in my life, and I trotted out my story of restless wandering and uncertainty. Then he did something remarkable. He told me that he would pray for me and then prayed, right then and there, on the phone. It was the first time anyone had stopped our conversation and my own self-centred spiral to speak to God openly about it. No lightning bolt struck from heaven, but we ended the call and I decided to visit the Brooklyn Tabernacle that afternoon. If you've never heard of this place, put this book down and buy any book by Jim Cymbala and read it twice. I turned up in shorts and a tank top, and swiftly realized that I was underdressed, so I went to a local charity shop and bought a dress, to feel a bit more as though I cared about entering the house of God on a Sunday afternoon.

Brooklyn Tabernacle swayed. We sang, and danced, and cried, and worshipped, and a young woman stood up to share a testimony. She spoke about being called to the Middle East and said something like this: 'There are places only you can go, people only you can reach. Go to them with the good news of Jesus.' Then, like a lightning bolt, God spoke to me: 'For a little while, you are still young and relevant in a way that I can use with young people. Go back to the church where you grew up and work with the teenagers there.'

So I did.

Two things changed my direction in this story. The first was the simple power of prayer. Prayer is intimate conversation with God. Prayer is intercession, 'knocking on the doors of heaven with bruised knuckles' (Buttrick, 1942). Prayer is laughter and song, delight and joy in the presence of the one who made us. Prayer is listening and speaking, light and darkness, quiet and action, fierce and gentle. Learn to pray, and expect that your life will be shaped by the conversation you have with God. Many excellent books have been written on this reality, but I find it most simply described in the way Jesus instructs us in Matthew 7.7:

'Ask, and it will be given to you; seek, and you will find; knock, and it will be opened to you.'

The second change in my direction was in worship. When we have run out of prayers and courage and words, God meets us in the silence. Worship is the act of seeing our God as King of our hearts and lives. Worship can be song, dance, art, joy, tears, simple listening. When we make space in our lives to worship, to recognize that there is a God and it is not us, we find that our lives are reordered. In a world that is continually shaken, I am reminded of the beautiful description in Hebrews 12.28: 'Therefore let us be grateful for receiving a kingdom that cannot be shaken, and thus let us offer to God acceptable worship, with reverence and awe.'

In times of questioning, I have often found that a prayer map is helpful as I seek direction. This is simply a place where I write down all my possible options, the pathways ahead of me, and draw out the ways that I can choose to walk forwards. Often we find ourselves in a place where we cannot choose the best way forwards, and occasionally we find that our lives are on a long detour. I am deeply thankful that 'his grace redeems our detours' (Mulholland, 2016). A prayer map provides the space for me to demonstrate visually the ways that I might be able to take the next steps, then yield my future and plans to God in prayer.

QUESTIONING THE CHANGE

My story is not neat and tidy, with every loose end resolved. Along the journey, there have been places of pain and question, and every change has included some loss. Your changes might mirror some of mine above or they might be a wholly different story. What should you do when you question the change and doubt the goodness of the God who has promised grace and glory?

Go back to what you know

This doesn't always mean that you return to your previous career or a previous love, but go back to the truths that you know, even if you don't feel them in the moment. In the Psalms, we read this reminder: 'Return, O my soul, to your rest; for the LORD has dealt bountifully with you' (Psalm 116.7). In the times when we don't *feel* confident, we need to return to the truths that are greater than our feelings.

Sink your heart into truth, not emotion

Our hearts are weary and restless. They can be carried away, like the tide, and suddenly we find them adrift. Sink your heart deeply into truth and guard your emotions from controlling your actions.

Listen first to Jesus

If you want advice, you will always be able to find it. You can find someone to tell you almost anything you want (within reason). Choose to listen first and always to Jesus, in prayer and through his Word, which is alive.

Allow your grief and know your wounds

Many changes include times of great grief and loss. Don't rush past that grief or you may discover that you carry wounds into your next chapter. Ask the Spirit for a genuine and deep healing for the places that are raw.

Seek joy

Alexander Maclaren (1895) said it best: 'Seek to cultivate a buoyant, joyous sense of the crowded kindnesses of God in your daily life.' If your future is uncertain, give thanks for your friends. If your job is uncertain, give thanks for the sunshine. If your physical health is uncertain, give thanks for your mind. If your heart is uncertain, give thanks for the unchanging Word of God, true even when we don't feel it. Seek joy and, sooner or later, you will find that it has been seeking you.

Spirit of the living God,

I want to be captivated, charmed and entranced by you today. There are places of change that are outside my control, and I have days when I feel that I am helpless and drifting. I pray that you would anchor my soul in truth; that in places of doubt I would go back to what I know; that you would open my eyes to the beauty of the story you are already writing in my life.

I take time today to listen to you. I see your gentle work in the wind, the trees, the beauty of nature, the intricacy of the people you have made. I pray that I would be more attentive to your kindness in my daily life.

I give you my times of change. I hold my whole life open to you and ask for a renewed sense of the crowded kindnesses of your love in my daily life. Thank you that, as a Father, you have loved me beyond anything I could deserve. I rejoice and receive your love today.

In the name that is precious above all others – in the name of Jesus,

Amen.

FURTHER READING

Cymbala, Jim (2018) *Fresh Wind, Fresh Fire* (Grand Rapids, MI: Zondervan).

Edman, V. Raymond (1984) *They Found the Secret* (Grand Rapids, MI: Zondervan).

Freeman, Emily P. (2019) *The Next Right Thing* (Grand Rapids, MI: Revell).

Greig, Pete (2019) *How to Pray* (London: Hodder & Stoughton).

Kendall, R. T. (1998) *The Anointing* (London: Hodder & Stoughton).

Koskela, Doug (2015) *Calling & Clarity* (Grand Rapids, MI: Eerdmans).

Merrick, Britt (2012) *Godspeed* (Colorado Springs, CO: David C. Cook).

Tomlin, Graham (2014) *The Provocative Church* (London: SPCK).

A ship in harbour is safe, but that is not what ships are for.

(Shedd, 1928)

Chapter four

NAVIGATING CHANGE

Our lives can change in a moment. In times of change, God cares far more about what kind of person we are becoming than what kind of things we do. As I've sought to become the kind of person who navigates change with grace, there are certain practical lessons that I've learnt along the way that have guarded my heart from shipwreck.

The Gospels trace a continual story of change: the change of water to wine, of fisherman to follower, of fear to faith, and, ultimately, of death to life. As in our own lives, the stories are not always perfectly straightforward; they carry an element of mystery, of the layers of decisions that can complicate our journey to our destination.

When I was younger, I always imagined that life would be much easier if God were to give me a very clear road map in order to navigate every decision. Because I was a good Christian kid, I knew all the scriptures about direction: 'Trust in the LORD with all your heart, and do not lean on your own understanding. In all your ways acknowledge him, and he will make straight your paths' (Proverbs 3.5–6). I would often pair that with the reminder 'Your word is a lamp to my feet and a light to my path' (Psalm 119.105), and simply expect that these two scriptures meant I could treat the whole Bible as my own personal Magic 8 Ball; shake it enough and I would be guaranteed an answer.

If you have been following Jesus for … oh, say, five minutes, you probably have already realized that life with him is slightly more involved than the shake-and-answer scenario. Alongside this, the Bible teaches us the *way* to live, but often doesn't speak to the particular outlines of scenarios we might face. This is why you can find clear teaching with different conclusions on questions like the use of social media, how to vote in the next election, sexuality, climate change and much more.

In this chapter, we'll be looking at some key principles for navigating change in the area of major decisions, mindset shifts and loss. Before we begin to consider any of those areas, may I suggest a simple answer for why God doesn't give us a road map? I believe it is because it is of primary importance that we are led by the Spirit. We read in Romans 8.14 that 'all who are led by the Spirit of God are the sons [and daughters] of God'. If the idea of being led by the Spirit of God seems mysterious, a little bit eerie and highly unusual, read on. Learning to listen to and follow the Holy Spirit has been a source of unending joy in my life. A guide is far better than a road map any day.

NAVIGATING MAJOR DECISIONS

I am asked on average once per day, 'Why in the world do you live in England?' I'm originally from Orange County, California, where you'll find the most beautiful beaches in the world in the land of eternal sunshine. I have a fantastic family who I adore, and most of them are still living in Costa Mesa, where I grew up. My answer, depending on my level of sarcasm and how much time I have to respond, is sometimes as simple as this: 'God told me to.'

That might sound dramatic, but it's true. I started visiting England in the summer of 2009 and never imagined that it would become my home. I loved the quaint houses, the charming accents, the winding roads that took me through green countryside and the aeroplanes that took me back and forth. I returned every summer, developing many friendships. Then I arrived for my six weeks in the UK during the summer of 2014, landing to the unexpected news that the leader of the charity I worked with had suddenly, shockingly, died of cancer. At times, you pray so relentlessly for healing that it almost fails to cross your mind that it might not come the way you expect it. In the weeks that followed, God spoke to me a promise from Isaiah 49; of a calling to the coastlands, a naming from birth, his word in my mouth like a sword, light for the ends of the earth. Sometimes, Cornwall feels like the ends of the earth, but in many ways it also feels like home.

The move from California to Cornwall was a significant one. In my own life, I received a word from Scripture, as part of my normal daily pattern of reading through books of the Bible, that particular summer in Isaiah. I then received the extraordinary confirmation of a friend praying that same, fairly obscure, passage of Scripture over me a week later. We had not seen each other in five years. Further confirmation included financial provision, the blessing of my pastor and boss, the encouragement of my family (who were not just trying to ship me off to another continent) and the general peace of the Holy Spirit in this major decision. Not every story is as clear-cut in direction, but I've found the 'Five CSs' from Nicky Gumbel (*The Bible in One Year*, 2019) tremendously helpful when I face major life decisions and change:

1 Commanding Scripture (the Bible)
2 Compelling Spirit (the Holy Spirit)
3 Counsel of the Saints (the Church)
4 Common Sense (reason)
5 Circumstantial Signs (providence).

My friend Olly Ryder first introduced me to this framework, and he expanded it in this way in a personal text in August 2017, which I found deeply helpful.

1 **Commanding Scripture** What does the Bible say about the course of action that I'm thinking about? Are there any verses that I'm drawn to?

2 **Compelling Spirit** Is there a sense of the breath, wind and guidance of the Holy Spirit in all this?

3 **Counsel of the Saints** What do godly people who know me think about what I'm proposing?

4 **Common Sense** God has given us reason for a reason, so that we can reason! Think through pros and cons, purpose and aptitude, interests and gifting, passions.

5 **Circumstantial Signs** Are there any interesting God-incidences around the situation?

A word of caution: don't use this as a checklist or a tick-box exercise, and certainly don't expect that every decision in your life needs to go through all five of these points. I still remember a friend who, every time I invited her for coffee, said that she would go to speak to the Holy Spirit about it. Apparently, the Spirit never said yes, but I wonder if at times she could have used number four in the list above.

As we navigate major decisions, we find great peace in knowing that the presence of God is with us. In knowing this, we are able to live out the reality of Philippians 4.6–7:

Do not be anxious about anything, but in everything by prayer and supplication with thanksgiving let your requests be made known to God. And the peace of God, which surpasses all understanding, will guard your hearts and your minds in Christ Jesus.

NAVIGATING MINDSET SHIFTS

Major changes can involve either our external circumstances or our internal souls. I have found that the inner changes can be more painful, because we lack either the vocabulary to articulate, the friendships to support or the framework to grow in our changes. Scripture cautions us against the kind of mindset shifts led by doubt. In James, we are told:

> If any of you lacks wisdom, let him ask God, who gives generously to all without reproach, and it will be given him. But let him ask in faith, with no doubting, for the one who doubts is like a wave of the sea that is driven and tossed by the wind. For that person must not suppose that he will receive anything from the Lord; he is a double-minded man, unstable in all his ways.
>
> (James 1.5–8)

The double-minded are easily swayed, tossed about by every wind of doctrine or opinion, shifting like quicksand. We can be trapped by ideas that seem convenient, fashionable or helpful. Douglas Murray (2019) identifies that we now live in a culture that can be driven by *The Madness of Crowds*, in which 'we are going through a great crowd derangement. In public and private, both online and off, people are behaving in ways that are increasingly irrational, feverish, herd-like, and simply unpleasant'.

A clear contrast exists between the one who is swayed by popular opinion and the one who, in genuine humility, chooses to consider new ideas and grow in grace. It seems no accident that so many of Jesus' parables speak of the kingdom of God as a place where there is great growth: parables of the mustard seed and the leaven (Luke 13.18–21) and the ever-widening invitation to the feast of God (Luke 14.12–24).

In many ways, my life and theology have been widened by my life in England. I have been introduced to a more generous view of the Church through my study at an Anglican theological university called St Mellitus. I have broadened my understanding of preaching and the roles of women in ministry after years of careful study. I have changed my attitude and approach to spiritual conversation. I pray that I have grown in grace.

In some ways, our whole life in Christ is marked by change. The word for repentance in the Greek, *metanoia*, can be simply translated as 'a change of mind'. We change our minds from being self-governed to acknowledging Christ as King, from self-confident to marked by humility, from self-obsessed to generously loving. This change of mind, or repentance, is not a one-time act. I choose daily to repent of the attitudes, ideas and actions that will harm my relationship with God and others.

As John Henry Newman says, 'here below, to live is to change, and to be perfect is to have changed often' (Ford, 2004). My life is far from perfect, but I believe that we walk in true grace when we are willing to navigate mindset shifts with wisdom and generosity. For many years, I saw faith as a fixed destination, a landmark, a statue commemorating all that is right and true, but increasingly I see faith as a journey, a conversation, an ongoing pattern of being shaped and reshaped into the image of Jesus. I still know where I am going, towards him, but I am far less concerned about 'getting there' and far more aware of this simple question: am I walking with him?

When I navigate a shift of mindset, I look at my questions in light of Scripture, in light of the life of Jesus and in active prayer. Rather than be a stagnant pool, unmoving and turgid, I agree with the words of Sarah Bessey (2015):

> I hope we change. I hope we grow. I hope we push against the darkness and let the light in and breathe into the kingdom come. I hope we become a refuge for the weary and the pilgrims, for the child and the aged, for the ones who have been strong too long. And I hope we all live like we are loved.

NAVIGATING LOSS

Every change is marked by some measure of loss. Indeed, as Rolheiser (1999) reminds us, 'every choice is a thousand renunciations. To choose one thing is to turn one's back on many others.' We navigate loss with the things that we choose to change, and we wrestle with the losses we would never have chosen.

Key chapters of my life have been marked by deep loss, great grief, unanswered questions. I have lost family, watched children I love suffer and die, experienced the ache of bitter prayers, the tears of impossible pain. There are no easy answers to the problem of suffering, and the natural bent of my heart is to hold on to what was. I've been deeply shaped by my history, relationships and legacy. I love deeply, so losing aches deeply.

I've experienced many changes these past few years:

- the loss of a pastor who was also like a grandfather;
- the loss of my identity as I moved cultures, countries and careers;
- the loss of privacy, as my life has been increasingly public in ways that I never could have expected;
- the loss of teams at various intervals.

In every loss, we decide what memories we keep and, in seasons of change, I see these tensions at play: honouring the legacy and past well, and allowing time to process the grief of what once was, while listening expectantly to the future work of God's Spirit, the one who does all things well, and says in Isaiah 43.19, 'Behold, I am doing a new thing.'

The first followers of Jesus experienced all the questions and wrestling of loss. The one they had pinned their hopes, their dreams and their whole lives on was gone. All they had left was an empty tomb, what seemed like an empty promise and a bleak future. What does it look like for us to hold out hope as we navigate loss?

I believe it begins for us the way it did for them: waking up and returning to the place where we last found Jesus. Walking in the darkness and releasing our own sense of expectation of what encountering him might look like this time. Recognizing that our tear-blurred eyes sometimes see a gardener instead of a king. Asking the honest questions, even when our words are stammered out slowly. Listening closely when he says to us: 'Don't be afraid. Far more can be mended than you know' (Spufford, 2013).

Resurrection hope still rises, not just on Easter Sunday. We navigate loss as we know the one who has conquered death and still mends hearts and souls in his presence with us.

Abba Father,

In so many ways I would choose safety. I would choose not to change my life, my mind, my friendships. I would insulate my soul to walk in careful quiet. Your voice is calling me to new places and, while I sense that any place with you is good, I am uncertain about the mountains and valleys ahead.

I pray for the clarity of your Holy Spirit to show me the next right thing. I pray for the strength to obey your voice, the confidence to follow where you are leading me, the joy of the Lord to be my strength. I pray that I would focus on your goodness instead of my questions.

Above all, I pray that I would trust in you with all my heart, not leaning on my own understanding. I believe that I will see the goodness of God in the land of the living, so I wait on you who are faithful to finish the work that you started in me. I rest in the completed work of your Son, Jesus Christ, and commit my life to you again. Come, Holy Spirit, and be my guide and peace.

Amen.

FURTHER READING

Afolabi, Ayo and Ruth (2018) *More > Direction* (London: SPCK).

Buechner, Frederick (2017) *The Remarkable Ordinary* (Grand Rapids, MI: Zondervan).

Done, Dominic (2019) *When Faith Fails* (Nashville, TN: Thomas Nelson).

Merrick, Kate (2017) *And Still She Laughs* (Nashville, TN: Thomas Nelson).

Mulholland Jr, M. Robert (2016) *Invitation to a Journey* (Downers Grove, IL: InterVarsity Press).

Spufford, Francis (2013) *Unapologetic* (New York: HarperOne).

Therefore, it was very unsettling to suddenly feel like a boat being tossed on the waves. I wasn't sad, I wasn't frightened – I just had too many feelings.

(Cliffe, 2016)

Chapter five

THE PACE OF CHANGE

One of my best friends and I had a fascinating conversation about balance. We talked about how we spend so much of our lives today in search of balance, trying to find ways to juggle our personal lives, our work commitments, exercise and the relentless drip feed of social media, yet appear calm and peaceful at all times. I told her that I was searching for balance in my life, seeking some Zen-like state where all manner of things are always well. She looked at me, laughed and said, 'It's when I'm off balance that I most know how much I need God's presence in my life.'

Life changes. At times, it seems as though we are sailing through peaceful waters, barely putting in any effort, gliding through our days. Even when circumstances change, they seem manageable. At other times, it's as if we're out in the surf, caught between a heavy set of waves, and every time we catch a breath, another wave comes in to pull us under. Between these two extremes, here is the practical reminder of Scripture from Hebrews 13.8: 'Jesus Christ is the same yesterday and today and for ever.'

This little line is preceded by the reminder to remember those who spoke God's word over us, considering their life and faith. It is followed by the equally powerful reminder that we should not be led away by strange and diverse ideas, and to allow our hearts to be strengthened in grace.

Psychologists say that we make our decisions from either the head or the heart; that one or the other will guide most of our thinking processes in seasons of change. In many ways, I am guided by my head; I read often, study well, investigate thoroughly. When it comes to chapters of change, however, I am guided almost entirely by my heart. My emotions flood in like a wrecking ball, and my present circumstances often become the definition and rule by which I make choices.

This verse in Hebrews is calling attention to a present reality, that Jesus Christ is unchanging, regardless of our circumstances, whether we are head or heart led, despite our emotions. This distinction is not affected by our gender; I know many men who are excellently led by their heart, and many women who are head led.

When the pace of change is fast, we struggle to catch our breath. Our lives feel off balance and we want to get both feet back on the ground, set a schedule, maintain order. At other times, the pace of change can feel snail-slow and we just wish there would be a shift in something, anything, rather than the endless same. This chapter traces two paths to change: when we need to learn to keep up and when we need to learn to wait.

FAST CHANGE: LEARNING TO KEEP UP

One recent season of change felt more like the pounding waves than peaceful waters. I started the year surrounded by an excellent team, the kinds of people who made me believe that almost anything was possible. For years, we had celebrated the volunteer ethos of a charity in the UK, with sacrificial investment from hundreds of volunteers who keep a large-scale festival called Creation Fest free to attend. Then, like a domino effect, four members of my core team transitioned into ministry jobs that (shockingly!) paid them.

I would have told you that my confidence was in Christ, not in my team. I would have expressed to you the unwavering expectation that I didn't put my hope in people. Until the moment I lost the people. Suddenly I found that my confidence rested far more in the individuals around me than I cared to admit. I was in a ship that seemed to be sinking, and I didn't know where to throw the lifeboat. The pace of this fast change meant that I spent weeks crying, days agonizing, hours fighting. I couldn't see the way any of this could be good, so I kept trying to anchor as much as possible in order not to feel so adrift and uncertain. This was months before our world changed drastically and the whole events industry reached new levels of uncertainty. At the time, I couldn't see how anything good could come out of such key changes and the loss of people I loved.

There are several stories in the Gospels where Jesus is shown to be a God of miracles. He raises the dead, restores sight, turns water into wine. In one of the miracles, which we find in all four Gospels, he breaks loaves and fish and feeds first five thousand men, plus women and children, and then the same again with four thousand. The loaves and fish are few, but the miracle is generous. I began to feel as though the miracle we were celebrating was the loaves and fish, broken and shared, but that, at some point, the miracle had become manipulation instead of confident expectation. How many times can you go out for a meal with Jesus, not pack enough food and then just ask him to break open someone else's lunch to feed you?

I had seen the miraculous in many ways. Generous cheques had arrived on our doorstep, visas had been granted in unexpected ways, people had provided the time, the creativity, the resources and the equipment at just the right moment. God had answered prayer so many times and in so many ways. I knew in theory that God was powerful, but in the midst of the storm it's easy to forget this and let fear flood in. As if he knew how forgetful I could be, the story after the miraculous feeding spoke directly to my heart and my head in this time of fast change.

Finding calm in the change

Immediately he made his disciples get into the boat and go before him to the other side, to Bethsaida, while he dismissed the crowd. And after he had taken leave of them, he went up on the mountain to pray. And when evening came, the boat was out on the sea, and he was alone on the land. And he saw that they were making headway painfully, for the wind was against them. And about the fourth watch of the night [between 3 and 6 a.m.] he came to them, walking on the sea. He meant to pass by them, but when they saw him walking on the sea they thought it was a ghost, and cried out, for they all saw him and were terrified. But immediately he spoke to them and said, 'Take heart; it is I. Do not be afraid.' And he got into the boat with them, and the wind ceased. And they were utterly astounded, for they did not understand about the loaves, but their hearts were hardened.

(Mark 6.45–52)

Several aspects of this story strike me as unusual: the immediacy of the disciples' departure, the intimacy of the time Jesus spent in prayer after the miracle of feeding so many, the way he was willing to be alone on the land rather than surrounded by those who might otherwise bring him comfort. I relate to the disciples feeling that they were moving forwards quite painfully, the wind and everything else seeming to be against them. In the middle of their darkest hour, it says, Jesus was coming, but would have passed them . . . except that they called out.

This does not mean for a moment that Jesus is indifferent. There is nothing in his character that would cause him to ignore those he loves, but I wonder what their lives would have looked like if they hadn't called out in their hour of need. Peter, one of the disciples on that boat, writes much later that 'the eyes of the Lord are on the righteous and his ears are open to their prayer' (1 Peter 3.12). Jesus heard the call of his followers and immediately spoke over them words of calm: 'Take heart; it is I. Do not be afraid.'

In the middle of my radical and fast change of teams, I began to pay attention to the places where the breaking was opening new doors, widening my opportunity, expanding my heart, and also where change was exposing the cracks in my own faith and within the infrastructure of our charity. This was not a one-step process; I have found that where faith and emotion are entangled, where my heart is invested, my perspective is not always clear.

I learned three key lessons within this time of significant change and transition.

1. Fast change requires faith

First, I learned not to react based on my feelings. We aren't called to a robotic faith, where we parrot the phrases we know we ought to rather than the ones that we feel deeply. Instead, we are called to an obedient faith, a yielded faith, a faith that prays like Jesus 'not my will, but yours be done'. The weight of the cross would carry unspeakable pain and eternal glory. Even Jesus had moments of looking at the situation ahead and asking if there was any other way, yet 'for the joy that was set before him he endured the cross' (Hebrews 12.2). Our eternal life with him was the joy, but there was still a moment when the pain required endurance. Our places of change reveal where our faith is based on truth and where it is based on feelings. In these places, our faith can feel like a battlefield.

I have fought against unexpected challenges of transition, loss and shaky foundations. Instead of expecting that Jesus, the God who overcame death, can overcome the impossible in my situation, I have, at times, been defeated in my emotions by something that I have allowed to be stronger than it actually is. I have created too much space for the challenges and too little space for God's power to be at work in my life.

If faith is like a muscle, fast change allows us to see where our muscles have been stretched and where they are sore. My faith easily extended to what I could see, understand and explain. It was painful whenever I could not see or understand. When fast change feels painful, let it be a gentle prompt to step back and ask *why* your doubts and fears are exposed by this particular change.

2. Fast change requires focus

If you could boil down your life to one simple vision statement, what would it be? Fast change requires a continual refocus on what is essential. Think about a fast runner who pares down every ounce of fat in order to run unencumbered. We pick up baggage along the way, some of it beautiful. We collect nice ideas, good suggestions and new models. Each of these things can be a gift or it can become an unnecessary burden in the race of life. This is why the author of Hebrews reminds us: 'let us also lay aside every weight, and sin which clings so closely, and let us run with endurance the race that is set before us, looking to Jesus' (Hebrews 12.1–2a).

I have learned how much I need to turn my attention to Jesus, over and over again. We live in an age of constant distraction. I just think I have learned this truth and then find that I am still the disciple in the middle of the storm, wondering why Jesus is walking on the waves. My first and primary focus is on knowing my identity as loved child of God. As Timothy Keller (2013) says:

> To be loved and not known is comforting but superficial. To be known and not loved is our greatest fear. But to be fully known and truly loved is, well, a lot like being loved by God.

It is what we need more than anything. It liberates us from pretence, humbles us out of our self-righteousness, and fortifies us for any difficulty life can throw at us.

My fears lose any power in the presence of an unchanging God. This truth is so simple, but it takes our whole lives to learn it. When I think that I have placed my trust and expectation for love in God and then find that my foundations are shaken, I must begin the process again. In some ways, the depth of my faith has come primarily from the shaking places. I have changed greatly; Jesus never has.

3. Fast change requires perspective

In the moments when I have been despairing or drowning, countless friends have spoken hope and expectation over my life, giving me a new perspective. When all I could see was the avalanche, they helped me to see the mountain slopes. In seasons of change, cultivate friendships that give you kingdom perspective. One of my friends says, 'Let's do some blue-sky thinking.' I love that phrase, because it reminds me that even when the sky feels stormy and the earth feels shaken, there are places of hope.

We allow our attention to be blurred at times of fast change. As the old adage goes, we can't see the wood for the trees. If you are in a chapter of fast and harried change, I would encourage you to set aside some time to reflect on three things.

First, what is unchanging about God? What aspects of his character are still the same in the midst of your time of change? How have you seen this in your life recently?

Second, what is still true about you? Who are you, in light of his love? During this time of change, what kind of person are you becoming? Does your character reflect the character of God your Father? Are you choosing to be led by the Spirit?

Third, what areas of fast change require your attention and what areas require your rest? Where do you need to hear these words from Jesus: 'Take heart; it is I. Do not be afraid'?

So.

Take a deep breath.

Focus your attention on Jesus, the unchanging God, instead of your changing circumstances. Invite the presence of Jesus into your chapters of change. And believe these words are as true today as when the shepherd wrote them:

Surely goodness and mercy shall follow me,
     all the days of my life,
and I shall dwell in the house of the LORD
     for ever.

(Psalm 23.6)

SLOW CHANGE: LEARNING TO WAIT

At other times, change feels

S
L
O
W.

We think that it might be easier if change happened like a domino effect, because then it wouldn't feel so late. This is partially linked to our idea that busy means important and hurry means happy.[1] We find that, in many, many stories in Scripture, change came slowly. Noah built an ark for a hundred years, waiting for the first rainfall . . . ever (see Genesis 6—7). Hannah waited 'year after year' for her first child, weeping bitterly (see 1 Samuel 1). David waited 15 years from when he was anointed by Samuel until he became king of Judah (see 2 Samuel 5.4 for the date of his anointing). There is a reason Habakkuk wrote, 'For still the vision awaits its appointed time; it hastens to the end – it will not lie. If it seems slow, wait for it; it will surely come; it will not delay' (Habakkuk 2.3).

What are you waiting for? A change of job? A change of hope? A change of attitude? A change of affection? A change of location?

---

1 For more on this, read John Mark Comer's excellent book *The Ruthless Elimination of Hurry* (2019, London: Hodder & Stoughton). He's covered it beautifully, so I won't try to repeat it here.

Some changes are promised by God. One of the most interesting stories of change and promise in Scripture is found in the life of my namesake, Sarah (Sarai in some of the passages I'll reference). She and her husband Abram had been promised offspring who would number more than the stars of heaven (Genesis 15.5). They waited patiently, expecting God's promise to be fulfilled, but after they had waited for ten years, Sarah decided to take matters into her own hands and fulfil God's promise by asking her husband to sleep with her servant, to 'obtain children by her' (Genesis 16.2). This idea was as unacceptable to God then as it seems to us now, and the consequences of this act are still evident in our world today in the enmity between the people of Israel and the people of Ishmael.

Despite Sarah's manipulative ways, 13 years later God repeated the promise to Abraham and said, 'Sarah your wife shall bear you a son' (Genesis 17.19). When Abraham heard this news, he fell on his face and laughed (Genesis 17.17). Sarah's response was the same – she laughed to herself about her worn-out body and its lack of pleasure (Genesis 18.12). Yet, more than 23 years of waiting later, 'Sarah conceived and bore Abraham a son in his old age at the time of which God had spoken to him' (Genesis 21.2). The impossible became true, the darkness became light, the hope became reality.

T. S. Eliot expresses this idea in his poem 'East Cocker', where he searches, wonders if his soul can wait without hope, without love, without faith, without thought. When change is slow, we wonder if we can wait without hope, without love, without faith, without thought. Slow change forces us to ask long questions about hope and expectation, about faithfulness and goodness. As a single woman, I have been told over and over again by friends that they are praying for my future husband. I have received prophetic words, pictures, scriptures and encouragement of his imminent arrival . . . but he seems to have been delayed.

Fortunately, I have never set my expectation on starting my life's journey with God as soon as I find a partner to shoulder the load with me, and while I have loved and lost, my heartbreaks have been tempered by seeing 'all things work together for good' (Romans 8.28) as I choose to love Jesus first. Places of slow, delayed or prolonged change often require the same attention as places of fast change, just with a different reality, as we live in the tension of prayers that *feel* unanswered.

Slow change requires faith

Like my namesake, I still tend to laugh at the promises of God. If you had told my teenage, home-schooled self that I would travel to 90 countries, write a book (the one you're reading!), live in another country, choose any career beyond librarian . . . I would have laughed. The book of Hebrews tells us that 'faith is the assurance of things hoped for, the conviction of things not seen' (Hebrews 11.1). If you can see it, faith isn't required.

Slow change involves having the faith to believe that a marriage can be healed, an abuse victim can be made whole, an addict can be set free, a promise can be fulfilled. Choosing to walk in faith is not choosing to walk in an ignorant fairy-tale land where candyfloss grows on trees and unicorns float by, breathing rainbows. Choosing to walk in faith is choosing to believe the overarching narrative of Scripture, that there is a God who is presently making all things new. It is having the faith to believe that the promises of God are still 'Yes' and 'Amen' (see 2 Corinthians 1.20), and where they are not yet, they will be.

In times of slow change, I trace the faithfulness that is sprouting in small places. If God has been like a gardener in my life, I look for the seeds that I know have been planted. I water these with expectation, hope, intimacy and worship. I seek the first sprouts of new life springing up and I nurture them with care. Don't let seeds of faith be trampled on, stolen, snatched away or choked out. Slow change requires having the faith to believe that the work of God is more than what you might see at first glance.

Slow change requires focus

When change feels slow, we can lose hope. I began exercising regularly during the start of the first COVID-19 lockdown. At first, my goals were easy: one yoga session and 10,000 steps each day. I started walking more difficult areas around the coast of Cornwall and shifted from yoga to cardio workout sessions. Five months later, I found myself walking the entire Cornwall coast, 422 miles of beauty and a few beastly cliffs. I started with slow changes, just one or two sessions to keep me sane when trapped in the house, and discovered that the focus which came with those small changes ultimately shaped a much bigger change in my health, fitness and state of mind.

Author and entrepreneur James Clear (2020) says, 'The most overlooked and underappreciated growth strategy is patience.' Patience isn't sexy or glamorous, it doesn't tend to win us any awards and it's certainly not a celebrated topic of dinner conversation. Yet over and over again, Scripture reminds us to pursue, grow in, even *wear* patience. Stay focused on the joy of small growth and 'Put on then, as God's chosen ones, holy and beloved, compassionate hearts, kindness, humility, meekness, and patience' (Colossians 3.12). Choosing small growth and patient focus can yield significant change.

Slow change requires perspective

The Johari window is a commonly used tool (see, for example, Transforming Leader, 2018) that reminds us there are four areas of seeing:

- known to self and others;
- unknown to self but known to others;
- known to self but unknown to others;
- unknown to either self or others.

It's used for personal reflection, for business models, and in therapy in order to shift perspective. In the midst of times of slow change, we often think that there has been no change. Our lives feel settled into the impossible now and we see no sign of anything different from our present moment. When we step back, we realize how utterly ridiculous this is. Our world is constantly changing. If nothing else, the second law of thermodynamics reminds us of the fleeting stability of our existence.

A view of slow change in the light of Scripture is not a simple reflection on what we know and don't know. It is a reframing of our stories of change (fast or slow) in the light of Jesus. Reframing our stories requires boldness, recognizing that even if we seek clarity our whole lives long, we will still be learning to see in new ways. As John writes in 1 John 3.2: 'Beloved, we are God's children now, and what we will be has not yet appeared; but we know that when he appears we shall be like him, because we shall see him as he is.'

My clearest perspective arrives as I look at the unchanging love of Jesus and allow my story, life, relationships and work to be reframed by his eternal love.

> *In our secret yearnings we wait for your coming,*
> *and in our grinding despair we doubt that you will.*
> *And in this privileged place*
> *we are surrounded by witnesses who yearn more than do we*
> *and by those who despair more deeply than do we.*
> *Look upon your church and its pastors in this season of hope*
> *which runs so quickly to fatigue*

and in this season of yearning which becomes so easily quarrelsome.
Give us the grace and the patience
to wait for your coming to the bottom of our toes,
to the edges of our fingertips . . .
Come in your power and come in your weakness,
in any case come and make all things new.
Amen.
(Walter Brueggemann, 2003)

FURTHER READING

Comer, John Mark (2019) *The Ruthless Elimination of Hurry* (London: Hodder & Stoughton).

Greig, Pete (2020) *God on Mute* (Colorado Springs, CO: David C. Cook).

Nouwen, Henri (1991) *The Way of the Heart* (San Francisco, CA: HarperSanFrancisco).

Rolheiser, Ronald (1999) *The Holy Longing* (New York: Doubleday).

Not everything that is faced can be changed, but nothing can be changed until it is faced.[1]

Chapter six

DESIRING CHANGE

I love pursuing change. I still have a childlike faith that our circumstances do not define us; there is glory in the end, the middle and the beginning of our chapters; our lives are part of a much more beautiful story than we ever dared dream. Although my changes have often come in unexpected ways, I can see in reverse that each of them became a thread reflecting grace in my life.

One of the prophets wrote about change in this way:

'Behold, at that time I will deal
    with all your oppressors.
And I will save the lame
    and gather the outcast,
and I will change their shame into praise
    and renown in all the earth.

---

1   This quote comes from an unfinished draft of a manuscript by James Baldwin. It was discovered when film director Raoul Peck got access to the manuscript and shared the quote in his documentary, *I Am Not Your Negro.*

At that time I will bring you in,
   at the time when I gather you together;
for I will make you renowned and praised
   among all the peoples of the earth,
when I restore your fortunes
   before your eyes,' says the LORD.
(Zephaniah 3.19–20)

This passage speaks of a remarkable change: from shame to praise. The follower of Jesus begins to have his or her whole life shaped into an act of worship to the God who creates and loves. The most important change is the one that happens in our hearts when we know and recognize the presence of God in our midst. The passage before this speaks about the God who rejoices over us with gladness, quiets us with love, exults over us with loud singing (verse 17). The image of God in his unchanging love for us is startlingly deep; the one who created heaven and earth loves us in this way. When we know and recognize this, it creates a compelling invitation for us to live in a way that looks more like him.

This chapter is about what happens when we desire change. We might be looking for a change of career, change of relationship, change of accountability, change of fitness, change of attitude, or change of location. The pursuit of these changes, hand in hand with the truth of God's Word, the freedom of the Spirit and in obedience to the will of God, allows us to walk into new stories with joy.

DESIRING CHANGE

As we consider the ways in which we desire change, we'll be looking at a character in Scripture called Nehemiah, throughout the book named after him in the Old Testament. Many men and women in Scripture desired change: Eve desired a change in knowledge, Jacob desired a change in position, Moses desired a change in speech, Deborah desired a change from oppression, Solomon desired a change in wisdom, Esther desired a change to freedom. The story of Nehemiah is one that focuses on the reason for change, the prayer of change, the boldness of change and the importance of faithful companions as we change.

All the right reasons

Here's the first big question: why do you want to see change?

Take a moment with this one; don't rush it. Be honest with yourself and your motives. Consider the reasons, the emotions, the voices of others and the still, small voice of your soul. If you can identify what is motivating your desire for change, jot it down in the margin of this book, a note on your phone, a notebook.

Nehemiah felt the burden of the heartache of his people. We read in Nehemiah 1.3: 'The remnant there in the province who had survived the exile is in great trouble and shame. The wall of Jerusalem is broken down, and its gates are destroyed by fire.' Nehemiah saw the great distress of an entire people, his own people, and he recognized the need for action. His motivation for change was to relieve the shame and trouble of those who required physical salvation.

If your motivation for change doesn't come from such a generous place, don't assume that I am suggesting you set it to one side. A healthy body can allow you to live with greater intention, so by all means exercise. A new career can afford you the finances to enable you to be generous, so consider wisely the place where you are investing most of your time (tied with sleep) and energy. Our companions are our greatest influencers, so be intentional about changes in friendship.

When considering a motivation for change, here are a few key questions that I have found helpful.

- What has catalysed my desire for change in this area?
- How did I arrive where I am today?
- Do I sense the Word of God, leading of the Spirit or wise counsel prompting me to change? How has this been confirmed?
- If this area changes, will I be the only one to benefit or will there be any benefit for others?
- What are the next three practical steps that I need to take towards this change?
- What one step can I take today?

Be intentional about the ways in which you approach change. Your dream may not be to write a book, but whatever it is, take a first step towards actually doing it. Then keep taking the steps that come after it.

Focused on prayer

It's easy to take a first step towards change and then find yourself embroiled in good advice, 'to do' lists, a series of possibilities. This is where Nehemiah speaks to me most clearly. In places of change, let your first priority be prayer.

If you're anything like me, you might be tempted to skim this part. 'Yeah, yeah . . . prayer. I do that before bed and meals; got it, I'll pray about it; in Jesus' name, Amen.' This is not the kind of prayer we see in Nehemiah. We are told that he sat, wept, mourned, fasted and prayed before the God of heaven (Nehemiah 1.4). This was no casual conversation, no timid offering of ideas. The agonizing desire of his heart was laid bare before God, and his focus on prayer shaped the way that he approached change. Ultimately, his conversation with God ended up shaping a whole nation.

Prayer is a conversation. If your experience has been primarily that you say a few nice words to God and then hope, at some point, you get a warm, fuzzy feeling, you have only scratched the surface of speaking to him. We see that, as Nehemiah spent time in intimate conversation with God, he approached his places of change in the following way.

- **Worship** Prayer begins with recognition of the steadfast love, the deep attention, the utter trustworthiness of God. It focuses on the unchanging nature of the one who knows the heartache of our world, is already at work and invites us to enter the work with him. It recognizes his ultimate authority and kindness in our story and in the stories of others.
- **Repentance** Every day, I begin my personal time of prayer with repentance for the heart and mind attitudes that have distracted me from complete faith in God. Nehemiah goes further and confesses not only his own sin but also the sins of his whole nation and the ways in which it has ignored the commands of God.
- **Asking** We are invited to approach God with the boldness of beloved children. Nehemiah asks for three things: for the attention of God to his prayer, the attention of God to those joining him in prayer and simple success. This boldness is neither self-confident nor self-focused; it's simply a follower of Jesus laying out his desire for change before the God who loves him.

In the places where you desire change, start a conversation with God. I am always surprised when I look back through old prayer diaries and find that God didn't just answer my big requests for change; he also answered the quiet whispers of my heart, the things that I would never have known to say out loud. If all this sounds a little bit overwhelming, Anne Lamott (2012) describes all of prayer as 'Help, thanks, wow'. Feel free to live there in your conversations with God.

Three years ago, I wanted a house. I had lived in England for three years, in quite cramped apartments above busy town centres. I moved seven times in the first two years. I wanted a place to unpack, to light candles, to set a table. I remember visiting friends in northern California and crying at the beauty of their house (and my own impatience over not having one of my own). Somehow, I never took the time to pray insistently for a house, but it was a whisper in my heart.

One year later, through a series of events, including the loss of two long-term team members and the arrival of 12 extraordinary summer interns at the charity I worked with, I needed a house. I walked past one with a beautiful garden and bay windows two minutes from our offices. It was like an oasis in the desert. Three months later, I lived in that house, in a bedroom with wooden floors, bay windows and a prophetic painting from my friend showing new life in the desert places. I unpacked, lit candles and set the table many, many times. Even though my prayer for change had been a whisper, it was heard.

Boldness

There are places in our stories where our desire for change requires boldness. Returning to the story of Nehemiah, we are given a key piece of information: he was cupbearer to the king. In other words, he had at least one place of influence. A friend reminded me recently that the person who has the most hope in the room has the most influence. Nehemiah, shaped by prayer and all the right reasons for change, acted in hope and boldness. We see a few key patterns in his story.

- **Keep doing the work** Until the time for change came, Nehemiah kept doing the work in front of him, showing up where he was expected (2.1).
- **Be ready to express the need for change** When the king asked what needed to change and why, Nehemiah was ready to express clearly the areas that were close to his heart and give the 'short version' (2.3).
- **Ask clearly** After telling the story, Nehemiah was clear about what he needed to ask for to bring about the change he wanted, and had a plan that he was ready to share (2.4–6).
- **Be bold** Nehemiah asked for time, letters of authority, building supplies and personal provision (2.7–8). He understood the scope of the change that he was requesting and he boldly sought the full range of resources required.
- **Honour God** The favour that Nehemiah experienced in this chapter wasn't something that he tried to take credit for (2.8). We honour God when we allow our influence to show his power and love. What power, influence, privilege do you carry? How are you laying it down for the sake of the kingdom?

Boldness can be like a sharp sword. Our 'big asks' can be misunderstood and mistaken. If you aren't clear about your reason for asking or your heart hasn't been shaped in prayer, you are far more likely to wound in your boldness than cut through to truth.

With two of the teenage girls I mentor, we have been growing in the area of bold and specific prayer. Instead of praying that God will provide money for Bible college, we have prayed for the exact amount still required for the next payment. Instead of praying for 'good results' in A levels, we have prayed for the exact grades required for university acceptance. Instead of praying for better relationships with family, we have prayed for the specific ways in which we want to see healing and growth. As we have prayed these bold and specific prayers, we have seen some answered *exactly* as we have prayed them. Others seem halfway resolved or partially clear. In a few areas, we are still waiting to see anything change, but the boldness of these prayers has shaped our hearts to expect more from our conversations with God than ever before. We believe the good hand of God is on us (see Nehemiah 2.8)

Companions

True friends are irreplaceable. In his book *Dream Big,* Bob Goff (2020) writes about friendship through the image of sea otters. He says:

> Did you know that sea otters hold hands while they're floating? It looks a lot like they're going out on dates with each other. After seeing so many sea otter couples drifting two by two through the water, I figured there had to be some reason for the hand holding. I dug a little deeper and it turns out the answer is simple: *they don't want anyone to drift away.*

I was sharing a few of my dreams with a friend and then asked about some of hers. She told me that many of hers had ended in daydreams, where she drifted away into ideas that were nice but impossible. There are many things that can cause us to drift away: lack of attention, insufficient confidence, not enough time, mindless entertainment. I wonder how many life-changing ideas will be lost to blinking screens in our generation.

When Nehemiah had clarity regarding what he was doing, why he was doing it and how he would resource it, he found his companions. He told his story in a way that invited others to join him, reminded them why the change was important and gave a clear way forward (2.17–18). Finding the right companions for the journey meant that, together, 'they strengthened their hands for the good work' (2.18).

My life and change would not look the same without the companions who held my hand to ensure I didn't drift away. Here are a few of the characteristics of my truest friends for you to consider as you choose your best companions for the change you desire.

- **They love God's Word** One of my favourite activities is to read Scripture with friends. My true friends love to dive in deep, ask good questions, find the places where the Bible surprises, delights, challenges and intrigues us. True change in my life comes as I am shaped by a truth outside myself.

- **They pray with me** My true friends don't just pray *for* me (although I am grateful for those times as well), they pray *with* me. I sat with a friend recently, unburdening my heart, and her simple response was: 'I don't know what to say, but shall we pray about it?' True friends speak to God with you.

- **They speak honestly** Some of my ideas for change have been rubbish. We need the kind of friends who remind us that we are not at the centre of the universe and some dreams are not worth pursuing. When you find friends who are willing to be loving and honest, keep them close.

- **They believe the best** If your life is anything like mine, you'll fall once or twice along the way. You will let people down and lose sight of the truth. The best friends choose always to believe the best of you and can help to remind you of where you lost sight of truth in your journey.

- **They see the world differently from me** If all your friends are the same, you might be in a cult or, at the very least, a clique. One of my dearest friends is very different from me – we see the world through opposite lenses in many ways – but I have found his friendship life-changing because he continually gives me a new perspective. Always attempt to find the other side.

- **They celebrate my joys** Occasionally, I watch a romantic comedy and am astounded at the false and surface friendships in which 'friends' betray and backstab. My best and truest friends are the ones who are most likely to turn up at my house to celebrate my places of great success or joy. They aren't stingy with their generous love.

When Nehemiah began the great work of change, he named those who had come alongside him to build the wall: Eliashib, the men of Jericho, Zaccur, the sons of Hassenaah, Meremoth, Meshullam, Zadok, the Tekoites and many more. Check out chapter 3 of Nehemiah. I considered naming my true and faithful friends who have championed my places of change, but the list would be too long and the stories could fill another book.

Nehemiah's story of change takes some extraordinary twists and turns. So will yours when you desire change. He faces conspiracies and opposition, finishes the initial task of rebuilding the wall, redefines the relationship of a whole nation with God, initiates a series of reforms. As we consider desiring the kind of change that doesn't just shift our own happiness but, ultimately, also shifts our hearts, I'll let his final words close this chapter:

'Remember me, O my God, for good'
(Nehemiah 13.31).

Jesus,

I pray for messy, raw, authentic, bold, world-changing prayers. I pray that I wouldn't desire only the things that will make me happy but also the things that will make me holy. I offer you my hands, my heart, my mind and my dreams. I pray that where I need to dream for bigger things, you would expand the limits of my imagination and I would begin to seek first your kingdom, knowing that you are the one who adds and makes new.

I give you the space to work in new ways in my life today. I pray for the boldness and the wisdom of Nehemiah. I pray that I wouldn't settle for what is good when you are writing a far better story than I ever dared dream. Unsettle my soul for lesser things.

In your name,

Amen.

FURTHER READING

Goff, Bob (2020) *Dream Big* (Nashville, TN: Thomas Nelson).

Lamott, Anne (2012) *Help, Thanks, Wow: The three essential prayers* (New York: Penguin).

Ortberg, John (2014) *Soul Keeping* (Grand Rapids, MI: Zondervan).

Portal, Pete (2019) *No Neutral Ground* (London: Hodder & Stoughton).

Tyson, Jon (2020) *Beautiful Resistance* (Colorado Springs, CO: Multnomah).

The light shines in
the darkness, and
the darkness has not
overcome it.

(John 1.5)

Chapter seven

LIVING IN THE LIGHT OF ETERNAL CHANGE

As I didn't grow up in the United Kingdom, but now live in Cornwall, most days I am immediately at a disadvantage. I think that I should use the elevator to take the trash out from my apartment. Then I discover that the rubbish goes via the lift from my flat. I ask for the restroom instead of the toilet, drive on the left rather than the right, wave at strangers and think that it's perfectly normal. Surely they want to be my friend, even if they don't consider themselves a friend already.

My best friend is Jesus Christ. This means that I am still taken aback, slightly shaken, when I hear my best friend's name used regularly as a curse, not a blessing. For most of my early life, I only heard the name Jesus in prayers and reverence rather than as one of the most common exclamations of anger or outrage. I grew up in California, land of plenty and sunshine, surrounded by Disneyland, with a pro-surfer youth pastor, encounters with Sandra Bullock at the airport, expectant faith in abundance.

I was 18 years old when I took my first major international trip to Australia (thanks, Dad!) and made three shocking discoveries.

- Not everyone loves Americans. This was before Trump, but before Trump, there was Bush. Both have fallen somewhat short of international adulation.
- Not everyone wants to be my friend. See above. This is still a shock to me.
- Not everyone loves Jesus.

Call me naive, but I *was* home-schooled for my teen years, after all, and I live up to a few of the stereotypes. I am now in my late thirties, still learning (for ever), but one thing I know for certain is this: Jesus has changed my life, not just now but eternally.

I can live without the comfort of American culture (I did move to one of the most rural counties in the United Kingdom, the centrepiece of the universe, Cornwall, where people hold actual grudges about what order you put cream and jam on scones). I can live without friends, although I would rather not. But I cannot even grasp the idea of my life without the presence of Jesus.

John's Gospel describes the arrival and eternal nature of Jesus this way:

In the beginning was the Word, and the Word was with God, and the Word was God. He was in the beginning with God. All things were made through him, and without him was not any thing made that was made. In him was life, and the life was the light of men. The light shines in the darkness, and the darkness has not overcome it.

(John 1.1–5)

Change brings chapters of uncertainty. We are looking for eternal glory, but we are finite creatures. As we undergo this change, we sometimes need to be reminded that God is both Beginning and End, Creator and Artist, Life and Light. Where it feels as if we walk in shadows and darkness, God's light shines into our places of fear and brings strength.

So far we have been looking at many views of change. This chapter will consider how we live in the light of eternal change in a temporal, physical world, where the light shines in the darkness and some days it feels as though the darkness has overcome it.

Paul writes about this eternal change in 1 Corinthians 15.51–57:

Behold! I tell you a mystery. We shall not all sleep, but we shall all be changed, in a moment, in the twinkling of an eye, at the last trumpet. For the trumpet will sound, and the dead will be raised imperishable, and we shall be changed. For this perishable body must put on the imperishable, and this mortal body must put on immortality. When the perishable puts on the imperishable, and the mortal puts on immortality, then shall come to pass the saying that is written:

'Death is swallowed up in victory.'
'O death, where is your victory?
    O death, where is your sting?'

The sting of death is sin, and the power of sin is the law. But thanks be to God, who gives us the victory through our Lord Jesus Christ.

I am so glad that Paul introduces this idea as mystery. I grew up reading Agatha Christie and Sir Arthur Conan Doyle, puzzling my way to truth alongside Miss Marple, Hercule Poirot and Sherlock Holmes. They remind me, in a very small way, of Paul's idea: that there is a truth which sometimes requires a bit of searching for. The obvious answer or explanation is not necessarily the best one. Mystery gives us the freedom to speak about eternal change in a way that reminds us the story is not yet finished. We are still finding clues along the way about what it means for us to be changed eternally.

Yet, we do have some clarity. There will be a time when we experience a great exchange, and trade our flesh and blood for something with a bit more longevity, our tents for palaces, our weary wounds for glory. This is an exchange made possible only because of the person and work of Jesus.

We sometimes limit this reality to the Christmas season, when we consider God in a manger. We carry the image of a baby, wrapped in swaddling clothes, sleeping among cows, surrounded by shepherds. The image has become commercialized; we picture a Nativity scene, a film joke from Will Ferrell, praying to baby Jesus in all his 6 lbs 8 oz glory, a hymn or reading. Anyone reading this who has been present at a birth will understand that the scene was probably less beautifully sanitized than the pictures presented to us, but we understand this very simple idea: God came to earth as a baby named Jesus.

Immanuel: God with us.

The promise of this story is that, in our places of darkness, waiting, of unknown, longing, our God came to live and walk among us. Let us remember that the God of the manger did not stay a baby. He is, as Jon Tyson says in one of his sermons, the God willing to get dirt under his fingernails.

In the incarnation of Christ, we enter this beautiful mystery:

The God who created the universe,
Who called forth the stars,

Made the oceans dance,
Breathed life into our souls,
Chose to inhabit flesh and blood, to live and walk among us.

Most of my American friends still find the UK a fairly magical place. They think that I bump into the Queen regularly (or at least Kate and William) and drink tea every day, and believe that the accents are utterly charming. They have at least half those things right, but the daily reality of life in a country not my own means that I have entered it as a journey, full of both joys and challenges. The incarnation gives us the reality of a God who came to live among us, to enter into our lives and, in doing so, know us in both the highs and the lows. It is the revelation of God himself among us and this is *good news*. It means he 'moved into the neighborhood' (John 1.14, MSG), understood the ordinary moments of our day, cared about the individual, revealed his love.

The cross is the ultimate revelation of the love of God. At the cross, not only did Jesus bear our griefs and carry our sorrows (see Isaiah 53.4) but he also ransomed our souls from sin and suffering, from a world torn apart, and restored our relationship with a perfect and holy God. But the story does not end at the cross, because the resurrection of Jesus Christ shows his ultimate and complete victory over sin, hell and the greatest foe of all: death.

I still remember the moment that I first understood the glorious power of the resurrection. I was in conversation with a lifelong friend, discussing what had shaped our lives and hearts most in the past year. My friend said quite simply, 'I realized that, because Jesus has conquered death, there is nothing he cannot conquer. The resurrection means that there is nothing too hard for God.'

Think on this. Rest your soul for a moment. Live your whole life here.

The breathtaking power of the resurrection reminds us every day (not just on Easter Sunday) that we are offered *new life*. As it says in 1 Corinthians 6.14: 'And God raised the Lord and will also raise us up by his power.' Resurrection life means that we are offered the chance to be 'born again to a living hope' (1 Peter 1.3), we are given power (Philippians 3.10), we sing for joy and have a hope like no other: our 'dead shall live; their bodies shall rise' (Isaiah 26.19).

What, then, does it look like for us to live well in the light of eternal change? How does this glorious, breathtaking truth seep into our everyday, ordinary moments of life, work, laundry, relationships, meals and social media?

FAITHFUL LIVING

Living in the light of eternity frees us from the responsibility of rushing the present moment for a result or outcome. This is one of the areas in which I am personally growing the most. I prefer to operate using checklists, schedules, action points, attainable goals. I have, at times, drowned those I mentor or lead with an impossibly long list of books to read, podcasts to listen to, ways to grow. A genuine expectation of resurrection change allows us to live faithfully within our limits, to recognize that God is doing the work, and acts as a reminder that all is grace.

Relaxing into this truth does not limit how much we care, but it does limit how much we carry. Much of my American Evangelical background meant that I expected resurrection truth to bring instantaneous change, like a fairy wand waved over the distractions and sins of daily life bringing sparkling order and new chapters. I heard so many testimonies and read so many books about this kind of change that I thought we could identify patterns, prescribe Bible verses like medication and, quite simply, expect that if someone prayed a four-sentence prayer with the right parts (acknowledgement, repentance, receiving, commitment), their lives could be transformed instantly.

I am no less committed to the beauty of transformation and the eternal power of the gospel of Jesus Christ, but I am now more likely to describe it as Tito Colliander (1960) does when he speaks of prayer and the long journey towards transformation: 'A monk was once asked: what do you do there in the monastery? He replied: we fall and get up, fall and get up, fall and get up again.'

Our faithfulness begins and ends with the faithfulness of Jesus Christ. This relaxes our need to build a checklist and simply reminds us to look daily to Jesus, for 'the life I now live in the flesh

I live by faith in the Son of God, who loved me and gave himself for me' (Galatians 2.20).

FREE LIVING

The passage we explored earlier in 1 Corinthians 15 reminds us in verse 57 that we are given victory through our Lord Jesus Christ. Where we would otherwise experience the sting of death in sin, and the power of sin in the law, we have, instead, been given freedom from oppression.

Recently, I listened to the story of Ray Hinton, who was sent to prison for 28 years for a crime that he did not commit. Through the work of Bryan Stevenson and the Equal Justice Initiative, he was exonerated of this crime, released from prison and wrote a book called *The Sun Does Shine: How I found life and freedom on Death Row*. The oppression of systemic racism kept him enslaved in unspeakably painful ways, yet he sums up his experience by saying, 'If you want to be free, you have to forgive. And I wanted to be free' (Bowler, 2020).

Free living is costly. It does not mean that we ignore or avoid every consequence of sin. It does mean that, every day, we recognize the past stings, weights and powers no longer define us. Where our identity was once *slave,* we are now free. The distinct reality of this freedom is that it is not just freedom *from* but also freedom *for.* As God said through the prophet Jeremiah, 'Have I not set you free for their good?' (Jeremiah 15.11). Our freedom enables us to live in radical and radiant grace, but it isn't for our sakes only; it is freedom for the world around us.

As Ray's story illustrates so powerfully, this can require costly forgiveness. We can spend our whole lives discovering how to live the truth of Colossians 3.13, 'forgiving each other; as the Lord has forgiven [us], so [we] also must forgive'. Eternal change frees us from the responsibility of correcting the sins of others and undoing every wrong and harm done to us, and it frees us for new life.

EXPECTANT LIVING

Finally, it makes us expectant people. I love spending time with friends who have grasped the joy of the resurrection. They understand that our lives are not shaped exclusively by the moment in which we find ourselves. They are in it for the long story, the hard hours, but they have a clear expectation that 'this is the promise that he made to us – eternal life' (1 John 2.25).

One of my friends, a fellow writer, recently commented: 'Christians always seem so happy! It almost makes me want to be one.' Granted, she has had a particularly positive experience (not everyone would agree with her!), but I love that her observation about the followers of Jesus she knows is that they seem to walk with a joy that expects, even if the moment is challenging, the end of the story is good.

In the book of Job, we read:

'Behold, this is the joy of his way, and out of the soil others will spring' (Job 8.19).

Expectant and joyful living changes the shape of our hearts from self- or circumstance-focused to eternity-focused.

God our Father,

I want the kind of faith that understands the depth of your work for me; it is not just for a moment but lasts for ever. I pray that, as I reflect on the incarnation, the cross and the resurrection, I would grasp in new ways the eternal truth and freedom of your life, death and power.

I think of one impossible place in my life today. I hold it open before you. I ask for faithfulness, for freedom and for expectation that you are presently bringing redemptive healing to what is beyond my own power and strength.

I hear this promise: you are able to do exceedingly, abundantly above what I could ask or think. I rest in the truth of your victory for my life, today and for ever.

In Jesus' name,

Amen.

FURTHER READING

Athanasius (318) *On the Incarnation* (Public Library).

Fitzpatrick, Elyse (2013) *Found in Him* (Wheaton, IL: Crossway).

Reeves, Michael (2014) *Christ Our Life* (Milton Keynes: Paternoster Press).

Rutledge, Fleming (2017) *The Crucifixion* (Grand Rapids, MI: Eerdmans).

Rutledge, Fleming (2018) *Advent: The once and future coming of Jesus Christ* (Grand Rapids, MI: Eerdmans).

ten Boom, Corrie (1997) *Love Came Down* (London: Marshall Pickering).

Wright, N. T. (2012) *After You Believe* (New York: HarperOne).

And Jesus said to them, 'Follow me, and I will make you become fishers of men.'

(Mark 1.17)

Chapter eight

CHANGING THE WORLD

I hope this book feels a little salty. It was written by the sea and I hope that some of the sand has slipped into the pages. I've found that the best parts of my life have been shaped by grit, by the things I never dreamed might one day be worth sharing and certainly never dreamed might be glory. When we fish for new dreams, we are often surprised by what we catch. Sometimes, in the heat of daily life, we lose sight of the beauty still to come.

As Sophocles is credited with saying, one must wait for the evening to see how splendid the day will become. Most of my days feel ordinary, although we all define that word in different ways. My ordinary days have certainly brought some extraordinary chapters of change. In telling of these chapters, I've searched for all the threads of grace that have woven California to Cornwall, large to intimate, publishing to festivals, feelings to faith. Look for the threads not in my life but in yours.

At some point, change becomes an invitation. For the follower of Jesus, the change begins within, as our lives, hearts, minds and souls are shaped and reshaped in grace. We begin to become a new creation, the old things pass away and we discover that God is making all things new – including us. Our desires begin to be reshaped, our attitudes are adjusted, our souls are restored as we become people who live with 'love, joy, peace, patience, kindness, goodness, faithfulness, gentleness, self-control' (Galatians 5.22–23a), and this becomes more and more evident.

When we experience this kind of change, the natural response is to invite others to join us on the journey. I once believed that an evangelist was an older person, preferably a man, usually with a microphone, who gave a clear invitation at stadium-style events for people to commit their lives to Jesus, usually by raising a hand. I would now describe an evangelist as the one who looks around the table, notices who is missing and finds a way to invite them to the table, even if that's just to take the next step towards feasting together. It's unaffected by gender, rarely includes a microphone, but it does involve an invitation to know the God who loves us and created us to know him.

The idea of sharing your faith, giving the invitation to change, being an evangelist and speaking about God in everyday places might feel a bit daunting, so here are a few simple ways I have learned in expressing a faith that I believe changes the world, one life at a time.

USE NORMAL WORDS

Speak about God in the ways that reflect your authentic experience with him. Use everyday vocabulary to speak about life, change, hope and your dream for a world shaped by love.

Sometimes I wonder . . . What would be the best way for an enemy of God to destroy the possibility of someone getting to know him? Probably by making faith seem irrelevant, extreme, ridiculous and super-weird. Probably by making people believe that faith is about following the rules instead of knowing a God who loves you. Probably by convincing people that they would need to clean up their act, use less colourful language, stop their drinking, quit their casual sex, abandon their jokes and forget their friends before they could ever spend time with this God or his people.

These things are NOT the gospel. The story of the gospel of grace, of a love that changed and is changing our world, is the story of a God who created every human being, loves us deeply, knew about the brokenness of our lives and loved us anyway. He didn't say 'try harder' or 'do better', so that we could earn his love. He sat with sinners. He was holy but ordinary, pure but present at all the parties, infinite and mortal. His love was through life and to death, and there is an invitation to allow him to know and love us perfectly for ever.

SEEK CREATIVITY

Any good invitation is made even better by a bit of creativity. We see this today in gender-reveal parties, wedding invites, prom requests. True invitation to change is often best given by having proper relationships, honest conversations, daily parables, compelling podcasts, quirky videos, surprising books. All of salvation is an act of grace, which means that all our best invitations to faith should be led by the endlessly creative Spirit of God.

Jesus gave compelling and creative invitations. He invited himself to the house of a noted tax collector for a meal. He invited a woman to give him water and then offered her eternal, living water. He invited people to consider their lives and their world through the power of parables, startling stories that revealed deep truth. He invited fishermen to leave their nets, sons to leave their livelihood, prisoners to leave their chains, the dead to leave their tombs.

I pray often that a whole new generation of leaders would proclaim their invitation to a world-changing faith with even a fraction of Jesus' creativity. I pray for baristas, plumbers, prophets, chefs, builders, preachers, lawyers, marketers, artists, drivers, cleaners and politicians to display the radically creative love of God in their lives. A world-changing faith grows from a personal confidence in the way we live in daily relationship with God, for 'In him we live and move and have our being' (Acts 17.28).

LIVE BOLDLY

When we know and love Jesus, are led by God's Spirit and have seen true change and joy, we become boldly confident, expecting that our God is changing our world, one day at a time. For many years, I shied away from faith conversations with friends who were not followers of Jesus. I found it awkward or tense to broach the subject at the dinner table. As I have grown in my own relationship with Jesus, I have discovered that my faith in Christ is at the centre of how I see the world. The lens of the gospel changes everything. I find that most of my friends are interested in hearing why I believe in God, what my faith looks like, how it has changed my life.

Like the believers in the early Church of Acts 4.31, I want to speak the word of God with boldness. True boldness is not brash. It can be gentle and humble, winsome in reflecting the love of the God who has won my heart and is still in the business of winning hearts, now and for ever.

CHANGE YOUR CHALLENGES

Let's be honest: our greatest challenges are often closely linked to our greatest opportunities. As we invite others to a world-changing faith, this is most closely reflected in the simple statement that the gospel is good news. The challenge for the follower of Jesus is to believe this and to invite others to believe the same. In the words of Miller (1986): 'The gospel is good news – indeed supremely good news – which believed and acted upon produces a whole new life of praise for anyone, no matter how corrupted, confused or damaged.'

Here are some of the greatest challenges that sharing faith can include.

- **Language and vocabulary** We face the challenge to speak of the deep things of God in a language that won't be dismissed instantly or misunderstood by a faithless culture.
- **Perception** The perception of many today is that Christian faith is old, cold, dead and boring, belongs to another generation, and ultimately requires a brainless allegiance that sounds ridiculous to the modern man or woman.
- **Confidence** Despite excellent tools, including Talking Jesus, Alpha and Christianity Explored, many followers of Jesus find it difficult to speak about their faith in their workplace or friendship groups, and even in their own homes. The faith that was once a public affair has become increasingly private.
- **Doubt** The doubts and challenges to faith are significant and are often expressed with a clarity and authority that can rattle our foundations and leave us feeling adrift.

It is in light of these challenges that we are reminded, 'the early Christians prayed and acted on the basis that the good news was true. There is no reason on earth, and certainly none in heaven, why we today should not do the same' (Wright, 2015). I have found that the invitation to faith gives us endless opportunities. Here is a list of just a few of them.

- **Timeless truth** The testimony of the historical Church is that freedom is found in knowing a God who does not change based on the fashions of each era. The truth found in Scripture is for all generations.
- **Living truth** Our lives become one of the best invitations we can give to people to take the next step towards Jesus, and in this way we become living epistles in our friendships and communities, known and read by all (see 2 Corinthians 3.2).
- **Confident truth** When we do choose to engage with the tools available to us, including an increasing range of podcasts, YouTube videos, social media tools, apps and published materials, we can become confident that our faith stands to reason and share our faith with assurance.
- **Convincing truth** If, as in many places, people do not know much about the story of Jesus Christ, a personal knowledge of the gospel gives us the conviction we need to be able to paint a bold picture of the life, freedom, hope and peace that can be found in Jesus.

There is a moment when we recognize that the change we have experienced is worth sharing. It's the difference between speaking of faith to our friends who already follow Jesus and finding the confidence to share about him on Saturday night at the pub. It's the difference between reading our Bibles quietly in our homes and publicly in cafés. It's the difference between praying half-hearted prayers for God to bless our food and exuberant, confident prayers for him to change our world. In many ways, it's the difference between a God who is far away, up in heaven, twiddling with our affairs every once in a while, and the God who is near and present.

Sharing our faith ought to be gentle, relational, winsome, yet confident, for, 'Since we have such a hope, we are very bold' (2 Corinthians 3.12). As we understand and share the story of Jesus Christ, we are compelled to share our faith not as a duty but as a delight. As Tom Wright (2015) says, 'It is vital that those who believe the good news work tirelessly for real and lasting change in individual lives, the Church and the wider world.'

A FINAL WORD

Change is possible because of the power of the Spirit of God. The same Spirit who hovered over the face of the waters in the first chapter of Genesis and brought light out of darkness, the same Spirit of wisdom, understanding, counsel, might and knowledge we read about in Isaiah 12. The Spirit who 'helps us in our weakness' (Romans 8.26) is the only one who has brought true and lasting change to our lives.

Whether you've known the power of the Spirit for decades or you've picked up this book because the world seems upside-down and a friend thought that you might enjoy reading something from a faith perspective about change, my best invitation to you is to take a moment, set this book to one side and quietly pray one of the most ancient prayers of the Church:

Come, Holy Spirit.

It's a prayer that God delights in answering. May you know the sweetness and joy of his presence in the chapters of change that have passed, and the ones still to come.

'For now we see in a mirror dimly, but then face to face. Now I know in part; then I shall know fully, even as I have been fully known' (1 Corinthians 13.12).

Come, Holy Spirit,
The one who makes all things new,
Leave us
And our world
Forever changed.

FURTHER READING

Graham, Billy (2000) *The Holy Spirit* (Nashville, TN: Thomas Nelson).

Jack, Ben (2018) *The Simple Gospel* (Manchester: The Message Trust).

Wright, Tom (2015) *Simply Good News* (London: SPCK).

Acknowledgements

To my family: thank you for loving me through many changes and inspiring me to love others the way that you have loved me. To the friends who are like sisters – Meghann, Molly, Kate, Adie, Abi, Brittany, Annie, Rozlyn: thank you for listening, laughing, dancing, eating and growing old(er) with me. To the Merricks and Camps: thank you for giving me a home to return to and teaching me to walk in grace. To many, many friends at Calvary Chapel Costa Mesa: thank you for teaching me to love Scripture and praying for me, and for the unending support. To Calvary Chapel High School, students and staff: thank you for going on the adventure of change with me and being a place of great gladness. To Brian and Cheryl: thank you for trusting, releasing and loving me so well. To every young man or woman I've had the joy of mentoring: you have taught me far more than I could ever teach you. Thank you for the privilege of letting me walk with you.

To Emma and Beth: thank you for writing with me. I can't wait to read your books and share your stories with many. To Kathy: thank you for reading and reflecting back truth to sharpen my story. To Elizabeth: thank you for finding me, patiently pursuing me and giving me both structure and freedom. To Lucas: thank you for challenging me to make doctrine dance and being like a brother.

To St Mellitus: thank you for teaching me the joy of the many ways that we follow Jesus, and reminding me to love God with all my mind. To Patrick: thank you for the generous time at Mother Ivey's in which to drop these words from my heart to the page. To Evan: thank you for reminding me that my change has been free of cynicism and always believing the best. To Loretta: thank you for inviting me to teach on change for the first time in Mallorca. To Tubestation: thank you for giving me the space to grow and flourish, and find truth in new spaces. To my Creation Fest team: thank you for being kind to me on my best days, my worst and everything in between.

To my best friend of all, the one who loved me before, during, after, for ever: Jesus. Your Word is a lamp to my feet and a light to my path. Your name is like honey on my lips.

References

Bessey, Sarah (2015) *Out of Sorts* (New York: Howard Books), p. 97.

Bowler, Kate (2020) 'Anthony Ray Hinton: The sun does shine',
podcast (available online at: <https://katebowler.com/podcasts/
anthony-ray-hinton-the-sun-does-shine>, accessed 12 January 2021).

Brueggemann, Walter (2003) *Awed to Heaven, Rooted in Earth: Prayers of
Walter Brueggemann* (Minneapolis, MN: Augsburg Fortress), p. 148.

Buechner, Frederick (1993) *Wishful Thinking* (San Francisco, CA:
HarperSanFrancisco), pp. 118–19.

Buttrick, George Arthur (1942) *Prayer* (New York: Abingdon-
Cokesbury), p. 263.

Chambers, Oswald (2017) *My Utmost for His Highest*, James Reimann
(Ed.) (Carnforth, Lancashire: Our Daily Bread Publishing)
(available online at: <https://utmost.org/classic/the-way-of-
abraham-in-faith-classic>, accessed 12 January 2021).

Clear, James (2020), '3-2-1: On patience, vision, and emphasizing
joy', The 3-2-1 Newsletter, 3 September 2020 (available online at:
<https://jamesclear.com/3-2-1/september-3-2020>, accessed
12 January 2021).

Cliffe, Nicole (2016) 'Nicole Cliffe: How God messed up my happy atheist life', *Christianity Today*, 20 May 2016 (available online at: <https://www.christianitytoday.com/ct/2016/june/nicole-cliffe-how-god-messed-up-my-happy-atheist-life.html>, accessed 12 January 2021).

Colliander, Tito (1960) *The Way of the Ascetics* (New York: St. Vladimir's Seminary Press), p. 68.

Comer, John Mark (2019) *The Ruthless Elimination of Hurry* (London: Hodder & Stoughton).

Ford, John T. (ed.) (2004) 'In a higher world it is otherwise, but here below to live is to change, and to be perfect is to have changed often', *Newman Studies Journal*, 1(2, Fall): 3–4 (The Catholic University of America Press).

Goff, Bob (2020) *Dream Big* (Nashville, TN: Thomas Nelson), pp. 67–8.

Gumbel, Nicky (2019) 'Five ways God guides you', *The Bible in One Year*, April 20, Day 110 (available online at: <https://bibleinoneyear.org/bioy/commentary/1227>, accessed 12 January 2021).

Harari, Yuval N. (2018) 'Yuval Noah Harari on what the year 2050 has in store for humankind', *Wired*, 12 August 2018 (available online at: <https://wired.co.uk/article/yuval-noah-harari-extract-21-lessons-for-the-21st-century>, accessed January 2021).

Jones, E. Stanley (1981) *Christ of the Mount* (Nashville, TN: Abingdon Press).

Keller, Timothy (2013) *The Meaning of Marriage* (London: Hodder & Stoughton), p. 95.

Kierkegaard, Søren (1997) *Journalen* JJ:167(1843)(18): 306 (*Søren Kierkegaards Skrifter*, Søren Kierkegaard Research Center, Copenhagen, available online at: <http://homepage.math.uiowa. edu/~jorgen/kierkegaardquotesource.html>, accessed January 2021).

Lamott, Anne (2012) *Help, Thanks, Wow: The three essential prayers* (New York: Penguin), p. 23, quoting Rabindranath Tagore.

Lewis, C. S. (1966) *The Problem of Pain* (London and Glasgow: Fontana), p. 16. *The Problem of Pain* by C. S. Lewis © copyright CS Lewis Pte Ltd 1940. Used with permission.

Lewis, C. S. (1996) *Mere Christianity* (New York: Touchstone), pp. 175–6. *Mere Christianity* by C. S. Lewis © copyright CS Lewis Pte Ltd 1942, 1943, 1944, 1952. Used with permission.

Maclaren, Alexander (1895) in *Dictionary of Burning Words of Brilliant Writers*, compiled by Josiah Hotchkiss Gilbert (New York: Wilbur B. Ketcham), p. 290.

Merrick, Britt (2014) 'Ministry from intimacy', YouTube, 20 December 2014 (available online at: <https://youtube.com/ watch?v=ZHDJjojQu44>, accessed 27 January 2021).

Miller, C. John (1986) *Outgrowing the Ingrown Church* (Grand Rapids, MI: Zondervan), p. 49.

Mulholland Jr, M. Robert (2016) *Invitation to a Journey* (Downers Grove, IL: InterVarsity Press), p. 30.

Murray, Douglas (2019) *The Madness of Crowds* (London: Bloomsbury Continuum), p. 1.

Oliver, Mary (2006) 'On thy wondrous works I will meditate (Psalm 145)', *Five Points*, 10(1 and 2, Fall, Spring) (available online at: <http://fivepoints.gsu.edu/excerpt/on-thy-wondrous-works-i-will-meditate-10-1-2>, accessed 12 January 2021).

Rolheiser, Ronald (1999) *The Holy Longing* (New York: Doubleday), p. 9.

Sandberg, Sheryl (2017) *Option B: Facing adversity, building resilience, and finding joy* (London: W. H. Allen & Co), p. 77, quoting Viktor Frankl.

Shedd, John A. (1928) *Salt from My Attic* (Portland, ME: The Mosher Press).

Spufford, Francis (2013) *Unapologetic* (New York: HarperOne), p. 148.

Tozer, A. W. (1978) *The Knowledge of the Holy* (New York: HarperCollins), p. 108.

Transforming Leader (2018) example of the Johari window (available online at: <https://transformingleader.org/johari-window>, accessed 12 January 2021).

Wright, Tom (2015) *Simply Good News* (London: SPCK), pp. 116 and 119.

FORM IS A SPIRITUAL
FORMATION IMPRINT
OF SPCK

As well as being an award-winning publisher, SPCK is the oldest Anglican mission agency in the world.

Our mission is to lead the way in creating books and resources that help everyone to make sense of faith.

Will you partner with us to put good books into the hands of prisoners, great assemblies in front of schoolchildren, help create small groups resources for our Home Groups website and reach out to people who have not yet been touched by the Christian faith?

To donate, please visit www.spckpublishing.co.uk/donate or call our friendly fundraising team on 020 7592 3900.